I'D RATHER BE ME
The Story of
My Unusual Journey

Jo Ayres

authorHOUSE®

AuthorHouse™
1663 Liberty Drive
Bloomington, IN 47403
www.authorhouse.com
Phone: 1 (800) 839-8640

Published by AuthorHouse 07/18/2016

ISBN: 978-1-5246-1732-5 (sc)
ISBN: 978-1-5246-1731-8 (e)

Library of Congress Control Number: 2016910879

Print information available on the last page.

Any people depicted in stock imagery provided
by Thinkstock are models, and such images are
being used for illustrative purposes only.
Certain stock imagery © Thinkstock.

This book is printed on acid-free paper.

Because of the dynamic nature of the Internet,
any web addresses or links contained in this book
may have changed since publication and may no
longer be valid. The views expressed in this work are
solely those of the author and do not necessarily
reflect the views of the publisher, and the publisher
hereby disclaims any responsibility for them.

A word of thanks

I'd like to take this opportunity to thank the Saginaw, MI and Cape Coral, Fla VA hospitals, for their commitment to my care and continued improvement. I'd like to thank my parents, Dr. Don, and my neighbors Pat and Ray for the immense support they have provided me. And of course, I'd like thank the many friends and people I've met on this journey, who have offered me a lot of encouragement along the way. If it hadn't been for all of you, my journey would have had a vastly different outcome.

To write a book or to not write a book

Before it was over, I would start to lose my eyesight. Once I would commando crawl through my yard to the front door of my house, and at times across the kitchen floor to the fridge because I could not walk. I would sleep on the floor because I was too weak to make it onto the couch. And after all of this and more, I would sit and think to myself, "Is this what it's like to die?"

Almost from the very beginning of this adventure, people have been telling me that I ought to write a book. But trying to motivate me by telling me I really 'oughta wanna' is really no motivation at all. Think about it for a minute, trying to get anyone to do anything because they 'oughtwanna' rarely works. However, I was provided tools to accomplish this task and soon after I was out of the hospital, I started journaling about my experiences. It was slow going, partly because the story hadn't happened yet, and partly because I do lazy really well. So I would tinker away at my story and I stalled. Until one day I was talking to a friend of mine who was in a recovery program for addiction and she told me that one of the steps of recovery is to give back. I thought about my time in AA and it occurred to me if I had stuck with that program I would probably know that. The truth is I didn't care for AA and could not imagine giving back in that capacity. When I got home that day it dawned on me; maybe my way to give back is through this book. Not only to say thanks to the countless number of people who have helped me since the very beginning, but also to potentially help, or entertain, people I've never met. All of a sudden the book wasn't about me anymore and that made me feel better and more motivated. If I can succeed in thanking, entertaining, or helping even one person then I've met my goal.

I need to explain the previous scope of my world so that people may understand exactly how much these events impacted me. In one sense I could say that these events were chronic in nature because they did not happen overnight, but, it could also be argued that when I finally gave in and asked for help...the need was both urgent and important.

So let me tell you some about my history. Shortly after earning a black belt in Tae Kwon Do I graduated from college with a bachelor's degree in Criminal Justice. Soon after graduation I joined the U.S. Navy. I was trained as a communications specialist and graduated 3rd in my class. I was stationed overseas in Italy and later in Turkey. I enjoyed my time in the military immensely.

After my discharge I hired into a global company as a loss prevention officer. In the first two years that I was employed there I received certification as a medical first responder, a hazardous material technician and became firefighter I qualified.

I recognized early in my career that in order to be of value to the company I worked for, I needed to be willing to learn, change, move and grow. As a direct result of that I moved quite a bit among various sites, once I moved to a different state, and once I took a rotational assignment in another country (rotational meant 2 or 3 months there and a month or so back home).

During my rotational stint I was offered a position within the company to become an Ergonomic professional, and I started earning my certification in that field when the company reorganized and left me with 40 days to find another position within the company. I landed, not in my milieu – which was safety, but in a position in a lab. I was thankful for the opportunity to try something new. I didn't want to leave the company – I had great benefits, a good-paying job and seniority. It was not in my genetic make-up to walk away from that scenario. Truth be told, I was not cut out for that job, but I tried to make the best of it. In 2012 the company cut 800 people. I was one of them. To this day I am not sure if I was more embarrassed or relieved by the situation I found myself in.

People have consistently asked me, "What happened?" and I sought a definitive answer. I had a basic need to put some semblance of order into what was tantamount to utter chaos. I have always felt that what happened to me was insidious- I didn't see it coming. If there was a pattern, or some sort of formula to make sense of it all, then I remained clueless and I felt unbelievably frustrated at my inability to communicate what I felt should have been easy. It wasn't until I talked to someone who introduced me to the concept of the downward spiral, and subsequently the upward spiral, that I finally found the answers I was seeking, well, some of them anyway. Thanks Dr. Don.

As for my particular downward spiral – the bad thing that happened was that I lost my job and wasn't rehired anywhere. The first display of something awry was when I'd plan to sleep for five minutes and get up five hours later. Call for help? And say what? "Hello, my symptoms are I'm tired and lethargic." The likely reply; "Join the crowd." It just wasn't troublesome enough. My trick knee giving me problems? It's been that way for months – no cause for alarm.

So losing my job was bad; not getting rehired made me feel worth less and with no money coming in, I felt hopeless. Add the gradual physical issues – my inability to walk, see, and drive and the sense of isolation was prevalent. Sitting on my couch wondering, "Is this what it's like to die?" was bad but it wasn't until I couldn't get on the toilet to pee that I felt utter powerlessness.

Not being able to get to and onto the toilet was what finally led me to my 'self-triggered transition' and let the upward spiral commence. This book is a great deal about the upward spiral.

The Descent – questions people ask

- ○ **Why didn't you call for help?**

I didn't call for help, in part, because I didn't know how sick I was. I had let it go on too long. I didn't realize how bad off I was until a friend of mine came over to help me write some checks, because I couldn't see well. She told me how bad I looked, that I needed medical help, and that I looked severely dehydrated. I didn't feel I had anyone to call. My parents were in another state and my closest relative was living two hours away from me. It never crossed my mind to call any of them. I had friends who lived closer but I had no intention of asking them for help either.

Being sick and needing help was as foreign to me as it was to ask for help.

○ **In hindsight would you have called for help sooner?**

As they say, "If hindsight were foresight we'd all be rich." Given the information I had ahead of the time – which was literally nothing – probably not. However, had I known how badly off I was – yes. The question remains; "At what point would I have known it was time for help?"

○ **Who would you have called for help?**

I still don't know. At that point in time I felt isolated and alone. My friends have families of their own who need them at home. I tried to be sensitive to that fact whether or not I was sick. The most likely candidate would have been Kay because she is the one who came over to help me write checks.

Blind ambition-:

When I initially started losing my eyesight I thought it was because I had recently started using over-the-counter glasses to read. I figured I was due for a real prescription; so this explained why I couldn't write checks, read a magazine or see my 70-inch TV clearly. I had blurred vision in the center of my sight which meant if I looked at someone in the face I couldn't see his or her nose but I could see either one of his or her ears. It wasn't until I drove to Walmart that I realized I couldn't see distance either. After that last trip to Walmart I knew I couldn't drive anymore. Of all of the things that happened to me during this time, losing my eyesight is what scared me the most.

On my last trip to Walmart, I parked near the cart return and grabbed a cart to use so that if my knee gave out I wouldn't tip over. At this point I hadn't eaten a lot of food, and I felt weak, but I had no idea just how weak I was. It wasn't as if I had skipped breakfast that day; it felt more as if I'd skipped food for the past week. I remember I wanted to get some juice and that was at the back of the store. I picked up some stuff along the way. After I got the juice, I started to make my way back to the front of the store and it hit me about midway that I would never make it without some help. I was so tired and weak that I had to sit down somewhere. Luckily for me there were some folding chairs as part of a display. I sat there until I felt strong enough to make it to the front of the store and the checkout line. I went through the self-checkout line but I couldn't manage so I had an employee help me while I went and sat in a chair in Subway. I had to go back, once they were done, to run my credit card and sign off. They asked me if I needed help getting to my car and I told them "no"; I would be just fine. I drove back home and didn't drive again. I figured it was one thing to go out; drink and be unable to drive but still another to start out impaired. That seemed to me to be more irresponsible.

During this entire time I rationalized to myself (also known as denial) that as long as I could pee I was still okay. In hindsight that was a really dumb thought. Somehow I figured that if my internal functions were okay I still had a chance to be just fine. I really thought I'd get better on my own. Besides, I had no insurance, no job, and I was living on money I had managed to save. I felt I had no option but to get better on my own. At one point, on an unrelated health topic, my mom had said to me, "Your health is more important, don't worry about the money." Sometimes in life we don't take our own advice. I figure that's why it's so easy to dispense it. It's like that saying, "Take my advice, I'm not using it." I'd like to think that if I saw a friend of mine in trouble, I would encourage him or her to get help, to the point of harassment. In reality, my friends didn't have that option because I never said a word, at least, until I couldn't pee.

After my difficult trip to Walmart I gradually lost my strength and balance. I started moving from my bed to my couch and chair in the living room by bracing myself on the wall or any piece of furniture within my reach. Eventually I could no longer get on my bed because it was too high and then I moved between the couch and the chair. As time went by, I just moved to and from my couch from the floor. I didn't attempt to get into the chair anymore because it was a swivel chair. I was afraid the chair would turn as I launched myself into it from the floor and I would hit my head on the wall. From that point on, I lived on the couch and floor. This was after I had tried to make it to my mailbox one night.

On my way to the mailbox that night, I stepped into the road and my right leg gave out. I heard it crunch as I sank to the curb. I debated attempting to cross the road, regardless of my situation, but then I recalled the video game "frogger" from when I was a kid. I remembered how bad I was at it so I didn't attempt to cross the road. I sat there on the curb for quite a while, thinking it was just my luck that I was stone cold sober and there were no police officers coming by to stop and help me back to my house. Eventually I commando-crawled across my yard to my front door, and into the house. That was the last time I walked without some sort of assistance.

During the time I was living on the couch and floor, I would scoot around on my butt using my arms to push me and sometimes using my feet to pull me. My friend Kay, the one who helped me write the checks the night I collapsed in the street, had dropped off some food. There were pretzels, a grilled cheese sandwich and various caffeine-free diet sodas. The night she helped me with my check, she told me I looked terrible and that I needed to get to the hospital. I replied I thought I'd get better, and if I didn't get better within a week, I would seek medical help. I was hesitant to go because I didn't have insurance. She told me that I looked severely dehydrated and reiterated that I needed medical help. She told me that if I didn't seek help she would take me herself.

During this time my neighbors Pat and Ray went to Walmart to purchase some items for me. I had written them a check and a grocery list. On it were things like eggs, lunch meat, tomato juice, cheese, bread, and mayonnaise. I felt these were things that would fatten me up. The problem was, I couldn't stand up at all, let alone cook eggs. I put the supplies they brought me in the fridge at a level I could reach from the floor. Eventually I managed to make myself a turkey sandwich by placing the items in my lap and dragging my body to the coffee table in the living room. I only ate half of that sandwich because I didn't have an appetite.

One night, I didn't have enough strength to launch myself onto the couch so I slept on the floor covered with a jacket. One thing that is new to a person living on the floor, and scooting about, is strategically placing things you are going to want in places that are easy to get to. It took a lot of planning to get them where they needed to be; for instance getting food from the kitchen table, or fridge, to the coffee table took some thinking ahead, and quite a few trips. I had nothing to transport stuff other than plastic bags or my lap.

It seems hard to believe now, but the truth is that from the time I started to lose my vision, became more lethargic, lost my strength and the ability to stand on my own, I kept thinking I would get better. Before any of this I rarely needed to go to a doctor; I was rarely sick, and I never went to a hospital unless I was the one driving someone there or visiting a patient.

I woke up on a Sunday morning and I had to use the bathroom. I rolled off the couch and scooted from there to the bathroom floor where I laid for a good long while debating the best way to get myself onto the toilet. It was an unbelievable effort to get my sweatpants and underwear down. I laid half on the toilet carpet and struggled to get to my knees. Once I got to my knees I tried several times to get onto the toilet but I couldn't. I didn't have enough strength in my arms to leverage myself up, plus, the pain from the weight on my knees was unbearable. I thought about using the tub to pee in, but I couldn't get to the rim to sit on it. My biggest fear was that if I fell in I'd never get out, I just didn't have the strength. In the end I managed to get an "overnight" menstrual pad from a drawer in the bathroom and relieved myself in that. I folded it up, wrapped it up, and placed it in the trash. I put another pad on in case I had to go again soon. I struggled to pull up my underwear and sweatpants, and as I laid there, gathering my thoughts, I knew I was beaten. I needed help. With much effort I crawled to my coffee table and after 6 attempts (reaching from a prone position to the surface of the table) I found my phone and called my neighbors.

As soon as I hung up the phone with my neighbors my phone rang. It was my friend Cheryl calling to see how I was doing. I told her my neighbors were taking me to ambulatory care. She offered to take me herself but she was 50 minutes away up north. Toward the end of the phone call, she indicated that my mother had called her the night before because my parents were worried that I had not been in touch with them. She wanted me to call her back when I knew where I would be that morning. I found out later that in order to contact Cheryl my mother had asked my uncle for Cheryl's husband's phone number. The two had worked together years earlier. My mom then called and left a message on Cheryl's husband's answering machine and the message was relayed to Cheryl.

Pat and Ray came over and assessed the situation; how to get me out of the house, where to park the van, and figured out where they would be taking me. I scooted myself along the carpet closer to the front door. They had backed their van up to my front door because there was no way I could walk out to the driveway. Ray had the good sense to bring a gait belt that he put around my waist to help me into a standing position. Once I was standing, I couldn't walk on my own so Pat put my left arm over her shoulders, and Ray put my right arm over his shoulders, and, little by little, we went out the front door, down the steps, and into the van. I was hyperventilating while maneuvering the steps, telling them that I couldn't breathe, so they stopped until I could catch my breath. During this effort, I remember Ray saying a litany of prayers. Pat would later tell me that they were shocked when they saw me, in part because my feet looked like "puppet's feet on strings, they just dangled around." They took me to the ambulatory care where I was admitted, had blood taken, and a CT scan. I knew I was dehydrated and I honestly believed that they would hook me up to an IV to replace the fluids I was low on and I would be out by late that afternoon. Roughly 4.5 months later I left the VA. Pat and Ray had saved my life. I remember on the way to the first hospital, I told them that I felt bad for keeping them from attending church that day. Ray responded that he knew there was a reason why they hadn't attended church Sunday. I was that reason.

After I was situated Pat and Ray left to run errands. Cheryl was there within 20 minutes and stayed the rest of the day. She helped me fill out forms, stayed in contact with my dad, and generally kept my mind occupied. The doctors told me my blood work had come back and that my magnesium was low. Another doctor came back and told me my CT scan had come back okay and she wondered if I had MS; but she was certain that I had some sort of blood disorder. In the end it turned out to be much stranger than that. They kept me there most of the day but it wasn't long before they told me I would not be going home that night. I was transferred to an affiliated hospital later that day.

After I had been admitted to the hospital my dad was contacted by Pat and Ray. Pat informed him that I was at St. Mary's Hospital in Saginaw and he needed to get there to take care of business as I was in serious condition. The first night that I was in the hospital, my friend Cheryl followed me to the hospital and wouldn't leave until I had contacted my father. She had been in contact with my parents from the night before and throughout that day. I was able to talk to my dad on the phone at that point; my hands could still hold the phone, and they didn't hurt. When I talked to my father that night he asked me if he should come to Saginaw. I told him not to worry because I had no idea what was wrong with me. I can't imagine what went through my parents' minds when they heard that their daughter who had never been sick a day in her life was in the hospital for unknown reasons.

One of the first things they did, after hooking me up to an IV in a machine that went "beep," was wash my hair. They brought out a bag that I can only describe as looking like Jiffy Pop. They put it in the microwave for 30 seconds and then put on my head. They massaged my scalp and it felt great. The next thing they did was give me a bath while I was in the bed. I was impressed as this was all new to me. I couldn't remember the last time I had showered on my own, but I knew it had been a while. During my stay they attempted to test my hands for electrical continuity and also attempted an MRI. I had informed them that I was claustrophobic. They gave me medication to minimize my claustrophobia but it must have worn off before the test began.

They were going to conduct an MRI of my neck and my head. They had issues with me moving my arms. I asked if I could put my arms down, so my hands would be near the ground. They said "yes"; but then they said I couldn't do that so they taped me in. That wasn't very helpful. Once they finished my neck region, they wanted to start the MRI of my head but when they did that, somehow my head hit something hard in the machine. I asked them to stop and when they did they told me they were about half done. I asked if they had started the contrast yet. They said they hadn't and I said, "Then you aren't half done. Get me out of here." Later on the supervisor came to ask me what happened. I gave my synopsis and told him that if I had been inappropriate then I would apologize. I also indicated that I had been told there was a larger machine available for people who suffer from claustrophobia. I told him that they had not mentioned it to me, but if they had, I would not have been receptive to it at that point. I was more than willing to try the MRI again when it was available. If it would help me I was all for it.

I spent the first night in that ward. The second night they moved me to another wing due to a highly contagious child coming onto the floor. Those couple of days are a blur to me. But I do remember waking up at one point after hearing my father's voice. I looked at him and asked him, "What are you doing here?" And he replied, "I was in the area and I thought I'd stop by." There was a lot of confusion in my mind about what was happening. I can't say that I was scared – I wasn't – and I still had use of my hands. Whatever had come over me wasn't done yet, but I didn't know it, and neither did anyone else.

I didn't know it at the time, but after Pat and Ray had contacted my dad in Florida, he immediately contacted the intake officer at the Saginaw VA in an attempt to have me admitted. It made sense because I had no job, no other income and I'm a veteran. He informed my father that I would have to make the application and until then, nothing could be done.

The next day my father arrived in Saginaw and learned the extent of my medical condition as they knew it. Which apparently wasn't saying very much, but at least I was finally under a doctor's care. My father found my home in bad shape, due to my lack of ability to take care of my personal needs and housekeeping. I had not been able to vacuum my home for weeks, and I hadn't been able go downstairs to clean kitty litter either. Had I been more lucid I would have been embarrassed, but by that point I had other things to worry about. I had paid my bills for October before I left, but my insurance premiums for my house were due within weeks. My dad took care of the minor household duties and found a home for my kitty while I was away. My dad had friends come over and help clean out my basement. The cat had run loose in the basement because that's where her food, water and bed were. I had given the keys to my house to my neighbors so that they could check in on the cat, and clean her litter boxes, but they were not up to cleaning the basement floor. I was transferred to Health Source in Saginaw Township where the daily rate was $1300 per day. My dad paid $1500 for me to be admitted and then the rate was down to $975 per day since I had no health insurance. I was admitted on Friday at 2 PM and received two hours of rehabilitation therapy. I didn't receive any rehabilitation on Sunday so it equated to $2925 for 3 1/2 hours of rehab, a room to stay in, food to eat, and help to the bathroom.

They ran cognitive tests on me, and tested my strengths, and at this point I couldn't feed myself. Somewhere between St. Mary's hospital and my stay at Health Source, I had lost the ability to coordinate my hand to mouth movement. I remember one of the OT personnel came to my room and gave me a bent fork to see if that would help me aim towards my mouth. It didn't help. I remember going to the cafeteria to be fed and it seemed as if all of the patients were so old. I remember Halloween was right around the corner and the caregivers were talking about the costumes their kids were going to wear.

At this point my father was trying to get me into the VA, and when one of the administrators heard about it, he was careful to point out to me that the VA was always like the last stand for patients. Everyone held out hope to be admitted, but the truth was, phone calls didn't get returned, faxes never reach their intended persons, appointments were never made, and basically, no one ever got in (there has since been legislation passed that allows for veterans to be seen by a 'third-party' when certain criterion have been met. This new legislation has been a godsend for me personally.)

So imagine that administrator's surprise when he came to me the next day and said, "I don't know who you know, but you are out of here." I was at lunch when I heard the news, which means my caregivers heard the news as well, and they were in shock. When they found out that my father had been a local TV celebrity and former politician for our state, they were impressed. Everyone knew who he was and wanted to meet him. In a sense that made me almost royalty.

I did not know it, but was not surprised to find out later, that my dad had gone to the VA hospital and talked with the intake officer to present my case. He was given a form to fill out with lots of questions about my finances. Dad had spent several hours on Sunday going over my bills and was well aware of my finances. He had also found my DD 214 which is the honorable discharge form one receives from the military upon completion of service. Also, I had been denied VA services the previous year, due to having too much money (again, recent legislation has changed this significantly). My dad was armed with all of the necessary information and returned to the VA. The intake officer told my dad to apply for a hardship admittance and he would walk the paperwork through the system. The next morning my dad received a call confirming my acceptance. I was transferred from Health Source to the VA facility that day.

As soon as my father left that night my caregiver, whom I would later nickname Skippy, asked me if I could stand for 30 seconds. I replied that I could so he wheeled out the scale to get my weight. I had no more stood up than I fell down.

That was the last time I would attempt to stand on my own for four months.

The rest of the intake procedure was a blur. I remember doctors from all over came to check on me. I remember the first time they took me to the bathroom and they had to use a Hoyer lift. I have to admit they were on the spot when it came to food, medication, physical therapy and occupational therapy. I was in the system and I felt as if I was in good hands.

The following are abbreviated Saginaw VA admission notes. The intent of this section is to relay the depths to which I had sunk physically by the time I first entered the health care system. I didn't know it then, but some aspects would get worse before they would get better.

On October 28, 2013 the Saginaw VA received a referral from Health Source to screen me for possible admission to CLC (Community Living Center) for rehab.

They described me as a 44- year old female, NSC (non-service connected illness) Veteran with a history of ETOH (alcohol) and B-12 deficiency.

Per the Health Source notes, I was single and lived alone. I had been admitted to St Mary's Hospital on October 20th. I arrived at the ER (emergency room) with a neighbor and complained of generalized weakness to lower legs that had gotten progressively worse, to the point where I was unable to walk and had been crawling around my house for the past several days.

I reported that I was unable to pull myself up onto the toilet.

Per notes, I explained that I had gone to get my mail a few weeks back when my knees buckled and I fell. I had been crawling to get around since then.

I also complained of visual loss in my central visual fields.

I told them that I initially attributed my weakness to poor nutrition, dehydration and stress since I had lost my job, had no money coming in, and had no insurance.

I was admitted to neuro progressive care.

I was transferred to Health Source on October 25th. According to the notes upon admission I couldn't stand up, I had a wide base of support, and I moved my arms in a clumsy pattern. The original diagnosis was acute cerebellitis (inflammation of the cerebellum), visual scotoma, alcoholic encephalopathy, ataxia (poor muscle coordination), alcoholic hepatitis.

The VA received a phone call from my Dad, who was in town from Florida, stating that I had no insurance and was paying $900 a day at Health Source.

The VA screening committee met that day, reviewed my patient information, and agreed to accept me for admission to CLC I that same day. They also documented that I would require assistance with moving up in bed or turning.

The following are excerpts from my medical record; it's not all inclusive because I don't believe anyone wants to surf through over 2000 pages of data, hell, I didn't, and it's my file. Worth noting is the fact the information I received was only from my stay in the hospital and nothing about follow up care. The excerpts are noteworthy for their own reasons, some are for the hurdles I faced and some for the milestones I would achieve. They are all very black and white and do not encompass what my stay there was like (I have added some comments when I felt some clarification was necessary). In the ensuing chapters I hope to add some 'color' to my experience. I'll let the reader be the judge.

The date they evaluated me was Oct 30th, 2013, from 9:00 - 9:45 in my room. I gave a synopsis leading up to my hospitalization; I'd had a "blind spot" in both eyes, I lived by myself, my appetite hadn't been the best in recent months and I described getting my mail when my knees buckled and I fell. I had been crawling around my home since then; best as I can determine, that lasted about eight days.

I complained of pain in both hands, especially fingers, "if I touch something it burns". (Author's note---this development is what I was referring to above. When I was first hospitalized I had no pain in my hands, by the time this evaluation took place, it was excruciating to touch objects, especially metal.)

I stated I was unable to feed myself because of impaired coordination.

Author's note---the following is an excerpt of the evaluation notes filed daily. It tracks the ability of the patients to do for themselves, or in this case, the inability to do for themselves. In a nutshell; the overall outlook was grim. The upside is that I had no idea how bad off I was; so my personal outlook was positive. In a future chapter I will talk about when I realized how bad it was. It came to me in an unexpected way and from an unexpected source.

When it came to the following situations or activities, these are what the daily evaluation notes focused on;

BED MOBILITY (sitting up/rolling over/shifting in bed)

BED/CHAIR TRANSFER

TOILET TRANSFER (This is emotionally, physically and mentally challenging --- and embarrassing)

SHOWER/TUB TRANSFER

LOCOMOTION ON/OFF UNIT

WALK IN ROOM/CORRIDOR

UPPER/LOWER BODY DRESSING

PERSONAL HYGIENE (brush teeth/comb hair/wash and dry hands)

EATING

For quite a while my daily evaluation documented that I performed none of those tasks for myself and that the staff did all of them for me.

(Author's note; the following are progress notes from my physical and occupational therapy team. Again, I didn't list them all, but I wanted to give a flavor of my skill-set at the onset of my recovery.)

Some of my impairments, in the case of decreased bed mobility skills, were that I required assistance for bed height adjustment, reaching/placing left hand on bedrail, pulling the weight of my body up, positioning my hands flat on bed, scooting to the end of bed, and positioning my feet flat on the floor. I required greater than average time for these tasks.

I also had decreased transfer skills. I completed sliding board transfers but I required assistance for all steps of transfer and body positioning. I displayed ataxia (poor motor coordination) and poor body awareness and demonstrated an inability to independently place my hands on arm rests.

I was deficient in completing personal hygiene. While seated in the wheelchair at the sink I performed oral hygiene but while I brushed my teeth (at one point I couldn't aim the toothbrush and the caregiver had to brush my teeth as well) I required assistance for body positioning and assistance for opening toothpaste cap, applying paste to toothbrush, reaching/placing hand on water knob to run water, sipping water to rinse inside of mouth out, and cleaning around my mouth. Three-pound wrist weights were placed on my wrists in order to decrease ataxia however; signs of ataxia did not improve, and the weights were removed.

While I was seated in the wheel chair at the sink I combed my hair but I required assistance for reaching the comb, combing my hair, and blocking my face to avoid poking my eyes with the comb due to displays of ataxia and poor body awareness.

While seated at the sink, I washed my hands but I required assistance for body positioning and reaching/placing my hand on the water knob to run water, reaching my hand to the soap, and drying my hands. When the paper towel was removed from my hands I was unaware, displaying poor body awareness.

(Author's note---the following was written by my VA social worker)

"Met with veteran and her father in her room to discuss discharge planning and the completion of the advanced directive. Veteran shares that the goal is to return to her home, if not able will reside with her father in Florida. Veteran plans to complete an advanced directive but due to her inability to sign at this time, will meet with notary for her to sign the document with an "X". Veteran and father appreciative of the contact and care given to veteran during this admission." CLINICAL SOCIAL WORKER Signed: 11/01/2013 (Author's note---this entry indicated that I couldn't write and signed with an X; but what startled me later when I was going through paperwork; I found the advanced directive and where I had signed and it didn't even remotely look like an X. It looked more like someone had accidently marked the page with some ink.

It wasn't until later that I realized that was my 'signature'.)

11/04/2013 On this date I asked to have all four bed rails up at night due to spasms, which caused my legs to hang over the edge of the bed.

11/04/2013 This was no 'close call'. I actually slipped out of my wheelchair and ended up splayed out on the floor. My right leg was bent at the knee which resulted in my ankle being closer to my butt than was natural. I was seen at the bedside post-fall. I stated that I had slipped out of the chair onto the floor and that my socks were slippery. I told them that I did hit my right knee and did have some pain on the outer aspect of that knee. A 1 cm round bruise area was observed, so they ordered a right knee x-ray to rule out fracture. They further noted, "She does have full range of motion of the right knee, her breath sounds are clear to auscultation bilaterally. She is awake alert orientated x3. She does have tremors of her hands. I will order ice pack to be applied to the right knee for comfort 4 times a day for the next 2 days." They also instituted a seatbelt for my wheelchair. I remember thinking, as I was sliding out of the chair, that I was too far away from my 'call-button' and I knew the fall was inevitable. In the moments immediately following the incident, before the cavalry arrived, one of the service workers passed my doorway and saw me on the floor. He asked me if I was okay, and when I told him I needed help he trotted down the hall calling out, "Miss Ayres has fallen! Miss Ayres has fallen!" Oddly, the line from Chicken Little popped into my head, "The sky is falling!"

The following are some notes from my initial attempt at occupational therapy (OT). I had decreased bilateral grip strength. I attempted, but was unable to complete grip strength training using DigiFlex, activity was discontinued. DigiFlex measures grip strength but I actually could not hold the equipment to complete the test. Using both hands I completed using resistance foam blocks at all levels x 15 reps x 1 set. I had several drops during activity due to evidence of ataxia. I required assistance for body positioning and to maintain grip on foam blocks. On the upside, I had no pain, and no complaints.

I had decreased gross- motor skills. I completed bilateral biceps curls with 1 pound resistance dowel rod for 20 reps x 1 set. I also completed bilateral biceps curls with 2 pound resistance dowel rod for 20 reps x 1 set.

I had decreased bilateral upper extremity functional ability. While seated at table in my wheelchair I completed reaching activity while wearing bilateral 1.5 pound resistance wrist weights. I used my left arm to obtain 14 cones from a stack positioned right of midline and stacked cones 31 inches away to left of midline. I required moderate hand over hand assistance for left side.

11-08-13

"Subacute Cerebellar Ataxia. Suspected to be secondary to alcohol abuse, however suspect nutritional deficiency likely etiology and will need to review records to verify work up to date." (Author's note---this was the first time I learned that my alcoholism was not the single cause for my affliction. I am not saying alcohol wasn't an issue, but learning that ALL of this wasn't my fault, was a huge relief. In the end they determined a virus had attacked my brain and the alcoholism had served to weaken my immune system.)

11-11-13 By this date a major concern was that I was having involuntary muscle spasms in which my arms and legs flailed out and hit the guard-rails of my bed. The nurses put the rails up because I was 'shifting' out of bed.

(I had no idea they ran a drug test on me- in hindsight it made sense; but at the time I was clueless. I passed.)

- AMPHETAMINES
- BARBITURATES
- BENZODIAZEPINES
- COCAINE
- METHADONE
- PCP
- CANNABINOIDS
- OPIATES

11-15-13 All team members spoke with resident regarding her fall the night prior. Resident stated that she had fallen after attempting to stand at bedside with assistance of Dr. Z and Deb W. Resident stated that Dr. Z had been present and performing a physical examination of resident during time of fall. Resident stated that after being asked to attempt to stand, her "knees buckled" and she fell to the floor. Resident verbalized that she 'had not stood at this facility prior to this event and still does not feel that her legs are strong enough at this point'. Resident currently does not utilize a walker. Joni, Physical Therapist has noted that resident is 'completely dependent' for standing and recommendations remain for resident to continue utilizing Maxi Lift and/or Maxi Sky for future transfers. Resident aware of her own limitations and continues to utilize call light for assistance. Resident is also aware of fall prevention measures. Resident verbalized understanding with continued use of Maxi Lift for transfers. ASSISTANT NURSE MANAGER Signed: 11/18/2013 09:30

11-21-13 An update on my progress. "Ms. Ayres has improved turning side-to-side for bed mobility. She uses the bedrails for assist. She is unable to scoot or to sit from supine. Staff continue to use the maxi lift to move her in and out of bed into her wheelchair or to the toilet. She remains continent of bowel and bladder. Continues to need to be fed due to inability to hold silverware, regular or built up, and inability to control ataxia of her upper extremities to bring the food to her mouth. Staff continue to bathe and dress her. Right now it appears that she is working at her highest potential. Will continue to provide passive range of motion and assist with bed mobility and provide care as needed."

11-25-13 Progress update, "Pt (patient) reports that she feels she has improved in her vision, and strength in her core, can feed self with finger foods with min to mod difficulty, continues to have difficulty with using utensils to feed self. She reports she can't use her cell phone secondary to not being able to see the buttons and or push the buttons (needs to use her reading glasses). She reports that she can assist with getting her shirts and pants on while supine in bed, cannot button or zip. She also reports that the burning sensation in her hands has lessened, now only feels the burning in her finger tips where prior she was feeling it in the whole hand."

12/13/13 This day was my first trip home from 12:30pm to 4pm. I utilized a STARS bus to go home and retrieve some items for my trip and to close up my home. During this visit I sat in my front living room, in my wheelchair, and looked around. The thought that went through my head was, "I can't do anything." I couldn't even move my wheelchair, strength was one thing, but I was also conscious that I couldn't feel my hands and didn't want to get my fingers caught in the wheels.

Around this same time my VA social worker, Staci, made contact with my father and he stated that he had done the following things in preparation for my discharge:

- 1-Working with a friend OT staff person using a "dummy" of veteran weight to learn how to roll and transfer veteran in and out of bed and other areas of the home;
- 2-He is adding a heater to the pool to keep it warm to help with pool activities;
- 3-He is getting list ready to have the following equipment ordered from the VA: electric portable Hoyer lift; hospital bed, outpatient OT/ PT/RN ready to

order once veteran gets established as a patient at that facility;

- 4-He is making contact with the Cape Coral VA to start admission process, he is aware that he cannot make the appointment without veteran being present but he wants the paperwork process to begin;
- 5-He plans to request help with veteran at the home from the VA and also plans to hire extra help if needed;
- 6-Father appreciative of contact made with American Airlines to get the assistance for veteran during her travel time and for the staff providing the care for veteran, and expressed how much progress that he has seen with veteran since admission.

12-12-13 Progress report, "addressed improving independence with self-care and feeding self, using utensils. Pt able to comb hair mod I, brush her teeth including putting tooth paste on brush mod I, ate chicken wrap independently, used regular fork to stab and eat broccoli able to eat 1 pc, however became frustrated and then used weighted spoon able to scoop and move to mouth with increased time using slow movements, displays difficulty with ability to grasp utensils, currently is using a full fist grasp which limits her ability to manipulate utensils with scooping and adjustments to mouth, not able to open milk container, able to grasp milk container with bilateral hands and move to mouth take a drink with straw, not able take spill-proof lids off or place lids on cups."

12-13-13 "Multidisciplinary meeting at noon today in the patient's room occurred, which included Dr. Hasegawa (Neurology), Dr. Slomka (Medicine), Staci Ferguson (SW), Jane Briceland (OT), and Dr. Zaccagnini (Physiatrist who dialed in via a conference call line) to review the updates on the patient's current functional status. Dr. Hasegawa explained the multifactorial etiology of her cerebellar ataxia diagnosis- -likely a result of a non-specific viral illness in setting of chronic alcohol use. Additionally, the neurology specific autoantibodies and work up for other causes such as CVA and MS were negative based on the recent MRI. Dr. Zaccagnini (over speaker phone) reviewed the rehabilitation goals with the patient and the progress she has made. Advised on a more definitive plan for her to relocate with airline travel by mapping out a step-by-step process in order to plan appropriately. Jane Briceland- Sauve (OT) who recommended continued rehabilitative treatment as the patient is making slow and steady progress. She has improved upper extremity (UE) & some lower extremity (LE) motor strength, though coordination is a major concern and area of treatment focus. Consideration is being made to re-engaging PT as long as the patient continues to regain some strength. This is being deferred based on the OT's recommendations. Staci Ferguson (SW) reviewed the updates on the travel plans with the airline. It was decided by the patient that she would prefer to delay her travel since she has been making steady progress at this facility."

12-18-13 Progress note: "Pt. response to treatment: Pt. wore B 1.5 pound cuff weights during feeding task for increased proprioception. Pt. continues to demonstrate good motivation and work ethic. At times Pt. was bringing mouth to feeding utensil rather than bringing utensil to her mouth."

At this point Mary from OT came in to observe me eat my breakfast and made the following notes: "Pt. consumed eggs, toast, lemonade, fruit, and hot cereal while seated edge of bed. She required MAX PA with set-up. She spooned eggs onto the toast with MOD PA. She folded the toast in half and consumed the egg sandwich she had made. She required MOD PA to fold the toast in half. She was able to drink lemonade once it was poured into weighted mug. She fed herself 3 spoonful's of sliced, canned fruit. She was Dependent to feed cream of wheat with milk and sugar. She was D to open pepper packet, sugar packet, and milk carton."

12-19-13 Megace ordered 800 mg daily as appetite stimulant based on IDT discussion (Author's note---this was ordered for me because my weight had dropped so low. I remember my dietitian told me if I lost 3 more pounds they would feed me via an IV. More on this topic in the more 'colorful' chapters to come.)

12-19-13 OT notes, "Pt. has demonstrated improvement: Pt. able to hold small juice glass in B hands and drink entire glass through straw with no spills or drops." (Author's note---the first time I read this while reviewing my record it brought tears to my eyes. To think that I was so bad off that this would be a monumental achievement still absolutely floors me.)

1-31-14 One last update from my VA social worker, "Met with veteran during week, her plan is still to return to Florida with her father. Her treatment has gone well. The decision to keep her here longer was a great idea. Veteran recognizes that this was a great decision for her as well. Anticipated discharge date is set for 2/22/14. Veteran will arrange with her father the exact date."

Other notable notes I found while reviewing my record.

2-1-14 Transfer to toilet using walker.

2-7-14 First able to wipe myself. True story – the first time I wiped myself I actually wiped the outside of the toilet bowl. I thought, "Man my ass is round, and hard." After that I learned to use wet wipes because, although I couldn't feel them with my hands, I could feel them on my 'affected' area.

2-21-14 While I was in PT working with Sandy, this was the first time I stood between the parallel bars without hanging on and without a harness from the ceiling. That is a moment that will forever be frozen in time for me. It would be months before I would walk using only a cane, but I didn't know that and it would not have mattered if I did.

The facility – a day in the life.

I can't speak to what everyone's day was like in the VA hospital as a patient but I can give the gist of what it was like for me.

My day normally started around 6 AM when the night shift would come in and check my vitals. If necessary they would give me a blood pressure pill. Between 6 AM and 7 AM the trash would be checked; emptied; and if they had time, the room would be cleaned. During this time I could hear the hustle and bustle of the day shift coming on. There were medications to be passed; blood pressures to be taken and patients to be readied for breakfast in the cafeteria. I always ate breakfast in my room and that normally arrived between seven and 0730. I never really knew what breakfast was going to consist of, because often times it didn't look anything like what I had ordered the afternoon before, but ultimately, I was happy to receive a hot meal. Sometimes there were eggs, and sometimes French toast, and on occasion, waffles. I could always depend that hot or cold cereal would be served as well. From late December on Mary, from OT, would come and observe my progress during breakfast as I attempted to open butter, jam, the wrapping on the straw, milk cartons, cereal containers, and any other containers associated with breakfast. It was also an opportunity for her to see my progress using utensils. This was important because for the first month or so, I could not hold utensils and get food to my mouth. They tried to implement utensils that had bigger handles and utensils that were weighted to help minimize the tremors in my hands while I tried to feed myself. It turned out those items were not a long-term fix. Creative, yes, but helpful – not so much.

Just after breakfast was served, the day shift would come in and take my vitals. Normally at this point they would tell me if I had any appointments scheduled for the day. These appointments could include OT, PT, CT scan, x-ray's, a toenail appointment, a haircut, and on occasion a doctor's appointment outside the VA, at either another VA downstate, or a local hospital for a procedure. At this point I would discuss with my caregiver the day ahead; if and when I got a shower that day, and if I had any plans for the day myself, such as visitors or activities i.e. bingo, card games, movies etc.

Just after 8 AM I would get my daily meds. In addition to my usual meds, in the beginning they would give me heparin for blood clots (because I wasn't walking); a shot of Thiamine; and Megase which was an appetite stimulant in liquid form – it tasted like Pine-Sol and milk. I found out later that a small dose of Megase was used as an appetite stimulant, but a larger dose was used as an antidepressant. I told my dietitian later that it must have worked because I was happy as hell to eat all that food! I was 120 pounds when they put me on the appetite stimulant. My dietitian added chocolate ice cream to both my lunch and dinner portions. He also added a grilled cheese sandwich to my lunch regardless of what was being served that day. I told my dietitian I liked to eat popcorn and he replied, "I don't care what you eat, just eat." When I was in OT it seemed I saw food everywhere I looked; red rubber therapy tools looked like large licorice sticks, cardboard looked like graham crackers, and yellow therapy balls resembled grapefruit. Once I was sitting in bed and I swore I saw cookie dough on my calf. I thought to myself, "How on earth did I get cookie dough on my leg?" I looked closer and realized my Ted hose had split and it was my skin poking through. I gained plenty of weight by the time I left.

One thing I learned pretty early on during my stay was about toileting. I couldn't get myself to the bathroom so I was completely at the mercy of others; for food, drink, and anything outside of my arms' reach. Dayshift was good about transferring me to the bathroom via the hoist; night shift, not so much. As a result I learned a good time frame to ask to use the bathroom. This isn't to say that they would leave me waiting, it's more of a recognition that there were more opportune times to ask than others. Take shift change for instance. Their shift change lasted 30 minutes and so the beginning of the new shift was not always opportune, especially in the days when the hoist was needed. On night shift they would use a bedpan to let me urinate. The bedpan was not always positioned properly, and as a result, I would mess the bed which resulted in the caregiver having to change my sheets – sometimes in the middle of the night. I remember one time they had to save my urine for 24 hours so that a certain test could be run. These procedures seemed to be out of the norm, and as a result, the caregivers were not always on the same page. No worries though – it all worked out.

Another issue with the bedpan was how long it would take for them to come back and take it away. Once, a nightshift caregiver refused to use the hoist and insisted I use the bedpan. I was so tense I couldn't use it and after 20 minutes, I took it out from underneath myself. 20 minutes later he stopped in to check on me, and after I told him I hadn't used the bedpan he said to me, "Better luck next time." An hour after that, I hit my call light again and this time I was able to use the bedpan.

After my morning meds I would try to take a nap, which I realize sounds odd, but in those days all I wanted to do was sleep. Support staff would come around from time to time to offer magazines, sometimes a doctor would stop by to update me on progress or to let me know I was scheduled for another test. Morning was typically broken up by a PT session and OT was typically in the afternoon. Lunch was every day at noon. I felt the food was pretty good (either that or I had been there too long) and I have to say there was a variety. They would come in the night before, or the morning of, and ask for my preferences from the menu they had available for that day. There were a few times that didn't happen, and even a few times when I would order one thing and something else entirely would show up. On the rare occasion when that happened they were very good about getting something I would like instead. When I was still a 'feeder' the caregivers were timely in feeding me. As I got healthier and able to feed myself I still couldn't open some containers and they were quick to stop by and offer assistance. I don't know that they were happy to do it but they never seemed unhappy about it. I assumed they were on their way to do something else.

Good caregivers are a special type of person. Most of them that I met were professional, kind and very compassionate. These were the caregivers that I interacted with on a daily basis for the four months that I was in the VA hospital. I miss them, I miss hearing their stories, I miss learning about their families and I miss making them laugh. Not all of them were in that category and I am sure I was not everyone's favorite, indeed, if anyone's.

It wasn't unusual to get the same caregivers day after day and after a while, we fell into a routine. It was as comfortable of a routine as I could get in a place like that. I thought it was nice that every day they asked me what I wanted to wear. I understand that perhaps it was to lend a sense of normality (or a sense of control) to the situation and bless their hearts, but unless I had somebody coming to visit me that day, I didn't give a rip. There was a caregiver, Jenny, who worked nights and anytime she knew that I was scheduled to be at another hospital early the next morning, she would come in at the beginning of her shift the night before and ask me when I wanted to shower. It seems like an easy question, but I did not want to shower at 11 o'clock at night, and I sure as hell didn't want to get up at 4 AM. So she compromised and she washed my hair and bathed me without me even leaving the bed – she started at 4:15 AM and was done by 4:35 AM. She was not going to send some stinky patient to another hospital. I loved that!

There was one caregiver, Scott, who was in his mid-60s. He liked to come across as a crotchety sort, as if he was impervious to a lot. I originally met him in the cafeteria. He would feed me my lunch, which always ended with a serving of orange sherbet, something he claimed to hate (the orange sherbet, not me). He claimed he only ate peanut butter sandwiches during his shift. So one day he walked into my room and offered me a potato skin (the kind that come in a snack-size bag) out of his pants pocket. I refused his offer and I said with a smirk, "A potato skin? I thought you only ate peanut butter sandwiches! What kind of bull shit are you trying to pull on me? Get out of my room." He chuckled as he walked off. Then one morning he was scheduled to be my caregiver for the day. That meant, of course, that he was responsible for providing my bathroom breaks and my shower for the day. He asked me in the morning if I minded him giving me a shower and I said, "Hell, if you don't mind I don't mind". At this point modesty was really not an issue. He left my room and didn't come back for four hours. He told me he wasn't comfortable giving me a shower. I thanked him for his honesty and that was that. I found out later from different care giver that I was the same age as his daughter and that he just wasn't comfortable with me in that state.

One of my caregivers, Janine, confided in me at one point that she had been nervous about working with me because we were the same age. However, we got along extremely well, and I think in the end she took a special interest in me because I was her age.

There was a caregiver in particular who caused me to wonder if any of his patients thought he cared about them. One night I was using the trapeze over my bed to lift myself and scoot closer to the head of the bed. I said to the caregiver, "See, I'm getting stronger." To which he replied, "Well, that's what you're here for isn't it?" And another time he said to me, "Well it's not supposed to be fun in here forever." I remember thinking to myself at the time, "What part of this, exactly, do you think is fun?" But you never want to upset them because you are in their care and they can make it rough.

One caregiver, Debbie, would always come on shift at 4 o'clock and while I was still a "feeder" she was normally assigned to me for that evening. She would always make sure that I had pajamas for the night. I would ask her for a foot massage every night after she took off my Ted hose. Her response was always the same, "In your dreams". As time went by she would often offer me grape juice for my nighttime snack because she knew it was my favorite. It was the one thing I couldn't get from the VA store on my own, otherwise I had plenty of snacks that I bought with my bingo winnings. One evening she noticed that I had some kind of seed on my nightstand. When she asked me about it I replied, "That's your tip." She replied that I was too kind. So I told her if she kept up the good work, I would give her two. I liked to joke with her a lot but she also had some truly good feedback for me when it came to eating in the cafeteria with the other patients at lunchtime. At this point I could not control my hands, which meant feeding myself was nearly impossible (hence the term "feeder"). I could not cut my food; I could not take the wrapping off of the straw for my water; I couldn't use a spoon for my soup; and when I tried to grab a napkin it often fell on the floor along with multiple pieces of silverware. I was embarrassed for my own sake; but don't get me wrong, patients at the table were very kind and helpful and so were the staff. The staff would come and take our orders for lunch and the food was quite good. They knew I was going to need help and took it in stride. I was the one who had an issue with being impaired. So one evening Debbie asked me why I didn't want to eat in the cafeteria. I told her how embarrassed I was and that I felt like everyone was staring at me. This did not fit well with my "flying under the radar" mode. Then she said to me, "Do you really think you are so different from the rest of them?" She was right of course; and I had to face again that it wasn't about me. She was encouraged by my progress, after all, she had been the caregiver the night I fell on my head while trying to stand up from my bed at the behest of a doctor. She reminded me one day that when I left to live with my parents, it wouldn't be just a big change for me, but a major change in their lifestyle as well – in other words, cut them some slack. One of the great things about being monitored in the VA hospital is not only do they document your vitals approximately 4 times a day, along with the meds you take, but they also monitor your toilet habits. While this is no fun for the patient, I can't imagine that it's any fun for the caregiver either; especially when things don't go as planned. It seemed that while Debbie monitored my daily "habits" she invariably had to make use of the working end of a plunger. She would tell me, "You are the only patient I know who poops sideways." A few nights before I left the hospital she reminded me, "Tell your dad to go down to the hardware store and buy a heavy duty plunger". She was a lot of fun and very warm hearted.

I didn't have a nickname for Debbie but I had nicknames for more than one of them. The first person I nicknamed was Linda, one of the nurses who passed my meds. Due to the fact I was lacking in nearly every vital vitamin, the doctors had prescribed potassium four times a day (or maybe it just seemed like four times a day, regardless, it was a lot). As a result, every time I saw this woman it seemed as if she had another dose of potassium for me. I quickly nicknamed her "nurse potassium". The reason this was remarkable was because the potassium pills were huge. Most of the time she would cut the pill in half and even then she would try to mask the flavor by putting it in vanilla pudding. If I didn't swallow the pill immediately, it would start to dissolve in my mouth; the taste was awful.

It turned out that "nurse potassium" had a great sense of humor. The first three months I was in the hospital I could not "toilet" myself so in my room they had sling of sorts that they would secure around me and attach to a Hoyer lift – this wasn't just for toileting but also any time they needed to get me into a chair. The first time they used this device I was more than a little bit wary, but I had a caregiver who knew what she was doing, and I arrived at my destination safely. This wasn't always the case of course, because they had so few female patients to work with, and as a result, they didn't always secure me in the same fashion or have an accurate and comfortable landing. Once I got used to the sling, I mentioned to "nurse potassium" that they could liven things up a bit if they would just line the sling edges with pink fur. Although that got a laugh it was never implemented.

Skippy;

I nicknamed Mark "Skippy" because he really does look like the guy on the side of the peanut jar. He was a football fan and a basketball fan. When Mark was on duty he would stop by often, always with a smile on his face, and consistently in a good mood. He was fun and he taught me some of the rules of basketball, at least enough for me to be able to enjoy it while I watched it on t.v. Sometimes he would wash my hair in my room and once he even washed my stinky feet. His comment to me was something to the effect of, "Don't you just feel better when you look nice?" I remember around Christmas I discovered some Oreo cookies, with the red and green crystals in them, in my bedside drawer. They were from Skippy!

Red Squirrel

The "Red Squirrel" was a nickname for Sue. This woman simply did not slow down. She was also very friendly, upbeat, and supportive. During my time in the VA it was rare that I would be out of my bed without some sort of supervision. In the beginning I couldn't even get around in my own wheelchair, and as a result, my room was someone else's idea of what neat and tidy looked like. It wasn't that bad, but when Sue was on duty, that place was tidy. If she had a spare moment she would often stop in to chat. I remember one time she and another caregiver and I reminisced about Saginaw from when we first came to town; the different stores; the different restaurants; schools etc. It was a nice walk down memory lane.

Mrs. Garrett

I nicknamed Judy "Mrs. Garrett" because she bore a resemblance to the actress on "Facts of Life" and also because her demeanor resembled that of a house mother. She was so attentive. She would come in midafternoon and ask me if I was going to play bingo that night, and if I were, then she would recommend that I get back in bed and take a nap. So I would agree, and she would hoist me back into bed, and sure enough I would fall asleep. She would clip my fingernails for me, she arranged to have my toenails cut, my hair cut, and she even plucked my eyebrows before I left to live with my parents. Sometimes when she still needed to use the Hoyer lift to get me out of bed, she would get frustrated with the controls and once she tossed them in my lap. I joked with her and said. "Do you want me to drive myself over there?" She shot me a look and I said to her, "You're so cute!" That just served to fluster her more which made me smile.

Holly Hobby;

I nicknamed Katie "Holly Hobby" after the doll from my childhood. I don't mean this unkindly, she's a wonderful person, very affable, but her demeanor just reminded me of Holly Hobby. She wasn't gregarious, more like a wallflower than anything else. I know she had a lot of faith in me because she told me that when I got better she wanted me to join her in a 5K walk held in May.

Swiss Miss;

I nicknamed Sam "Swiss Miss" for two reasons. First of all, she often wore her blonde hair in braids like the gal depicted on the packages of Swiss Miss brand hot chocolate. Another reason was because Sam seemed not just capable, but determined and steadfast. From what I could gather, she lived in the middle of nowhere, felled her own trees and cut them up for wood to use in her fireplace. Honestly, I'm not really sure that she cut down her own trees, but if anybody could, or would, she'd be the one.

Maytag;

"Maytag" was a nickname I gave Sandy, my primary physical therapist. She and I had a good rapport considering that when I would try to transfer from my chair to a workout machine, or to a bed for exercise, I continually kicked her in the shins. I never thought much about it (I really didn't know what my feet were up to while I wasn't looking) until one day she told me she was going to wear her daughter's shin guards from soccer. One day I wheeled myself into the PT/OT office for a session while she was still working with a patient and she told me to move further into the room (the PT/OT share a working space separated by equipment) while she finished up. I wheeled myself in, around the equipment, and started heading for the other door when she stopped what she was doing and asked me, "Where in the hell are you going?" I told her I was planning to head out the other door, but it was closed. She has great sense of humor and she and I laughed a lot. I nicknamed her Maytag affectionately because she liked to agitate, everyone, but especially me. I tried to tell her my nickname was LMI, which is short for Little Miss Innocent, but she never bought it.

Diane Keaton;

Mary was my primary occupational therapist. Her demeanor, her conservative dress, and her overall look just reminded me of Diane Keaton. When I first started working with her, she told me later, that she was at a loss at how to help me. At the time I couldn't touch anything with my hands, due to the burning sensation I felt, and my grip was weak. She also had a great sense of humor and we found a lot to laugh about especially in the days of my Megase use when I saw food everywhere. Mary is the one who introduced me to my "magic widgets" which were straps secured by Velcro around my wrists. They were supposed to help me be able to bear weight on my hands without pain. The first time I tried them on they worked. I think it had more to do with the power of suggestion than any medical, truly medical, benefit. I still have those magic widgets – as a reminder of just how far I've come and of those many people, willing to try anything to help me out in the beginning.

I had a few OT goals I wanted to reach before I was discharged. One was to cook a meal and one was to drink a cup of coffee without spilling it. To accomplish the meal prep and cook, Jane, a supervisor, took me to an offsite annex to help me accomplish this goal. It went well enough – though I made it way too spicy. I took it back for my OT/PT therapists to taste. It was too hot for them. The next time I saw Mary for OT we put water in a coffee cup first so if I spilled it I wouldn't burn myself. During that visit I asked Mary, "Where are we going to get the coffee from?" she replied, "From the cafeteria…where the food is." I rolled my eyes and said, "Really? Next you're going to tell me books are in the library and toilets are in the bathroom???" She said, "I meant where your leftover food is."

Another time she was having me work on my dexterity when she asked me to take the cap off my water bottle. I unscrewed it. Then she asked me to put it back on. So I gently rested it back on the bottle. She said, "That's not what I meant." To which I replied, "But that's what you said."

Is it any wonder they didn't believe my nickname was Little Miss Innocent??

The Players – Visitors

☐ My Dad – reassurance

My dad was technically my first visitor since he was the driving force to get me admitted to the VA hospital. Once he was confident that I was under good care at the VA and we had completed my advance directive (the directive was a lot of words to describe who would be acting on my behalf in the event I wasn't able to make my wishes known – that would be him) he went back to Florida.

☐ Tom/Mary Lou – candy/popcorn

Tom and Mary Lou were some of my first visitors at the VA, in part because Tom and his son-in-law were the people my dad had help clean my basement. It was no easy task because the floor was a mess. I had my cat put in the basement with water and food (and litter) but she was anxious and upset. She showed it. Poor cat!

My mom had taught school with Mary Lou so I had known them for many years. They had also boated together so I knew the family as well.

They first came to see me when I was in Health Source and their daughter Michelle came also. Tom assisted transferring me to the VA from Health Source. Shortly after that, they were on their way out of state and stopped by to visit and drop me off some chocolates. From time to time Tom would stop by to check on me and bring me bags of popcorn. Tom is also the one who took me home on my day pass from the VA about a week before I was discharged. We stopped to pick up my taxes, pay my phone bill and he took me out to lunch with Mary Lou. We ate at Culvers that day. I remember because I ate chicken strips instead of a hamburger – I couldn't eat hamburgers without squishing the contents out the other end. Tom also drove Don and me to Flint Bishop Airport the day I was discharged and headed to Florida.

☐   Scott- candy bar

I met Scott when I was a college co-op at Dow Corning back in 1988. He and I worked at the same site and eventually he became my Tae Kwon Do instructor. Shortly before I joined the Navy I tested for (and received) my black belt under his tutelage. Through the years he and I had kept in contact although I hadn't worked out in his class since shortly after I had returned home from the service. I confided in him about my alcoholism one day. It was hard to do, yet it was easy, because he is a recovering alcoholic himself. Around the time of my admittance to the VA, he was in my neighborhood and saw my father pull my car into my driveway. He stopped to ask him if I was home. My father told him that I was not home and that I was in the hospital. Scott asked if I had suffered an overdose. My dad told him he didn't know. I am pretty sure that Scott left my house that day and made a beeline for the VA. Scott had a lot of business going on as a volunteer at the VA so he was able to stop by my room maybe once a week, for at least 15 minutes. He would bring me a candy bar and every now and then he would spring me from my room to take me to the pop machine where I could get my caffeine-free diet coke. I was surprised the first day he showed up at the door to my room, and I was touched that he would continue to visit me.

□ Cindi

Cindy is my neighbor from across the street and came to see me a couple of times. I never got to know her very well before this incident but I had known her and her husband before he passed away. I had gone to his wake. I never expected her to visit me. I remember her visiting in November and she said she would come back once the fields had been plowed but I never saw her again. I don't know what was going on in her life at that time but it was nice of her to stop by and show her support.

☐   Pat/Ray/Babe- pizza

Pat and Ray, the neighbors who took me to the hospital, came by to visit me at least once a week. Pat had taken over handling my mail, using my checkbook to write checks for my bills, and looking after my half of the duplex. During the holidays I got a lot of neat things from hospital volunteers. I gave Pat and Ray items that I thought they might be able to use – gloves, hats, watches, socks, and extra blankets that I felt they might enjoy. One day Pat and her sister brought me a pizza. I thought it was very kind of Babe to stop by. In the 13 years that Pat and Ray had lived as my neighbors, I had only met Babe a handful of times – probably less than five times. Pat and Ray and Babe would say prayers with me in the room, not always, but often.

☐   Nyla- subway/chipotle

I remember the first time Nyla came to my room. She is one of the most cheerful people I have ever met. I think I had only seen her once or twice before my hospital stay. I didn't know it at the time but she was a volunteer at the VA in addition to her own job. She blew into the room cheerful as could be, and full of laughter. I don't remember what we talked about that night but I do remember that it left me feeling good. For a while she would visit me every Wednesday night and sometimes she would bring me Subway or Chipotle. I finally convinced her to try Chipotle on her own and she said she liked it. I knew Nyla through my parents. I remember we laughed so hard that the nurses wondered what on earth we were talking about. After I had left the hospital, one of the nurses asked her how I was doing. I was pleased that they associated her with me because she's awesome.

☐   Gene/Mary Pat – Mackinac fudge

I knew Gene and Mary Pat through my father's association with the University where he used to teach. Gene and Mary Pat stopped in just to check on me and tried to help me decide what had felled me and left me in this condition. It would have taken more than one visit to figure it out but was a valiant effort. They had brought me some fudge from Mackinac Island on their way out of town for the holidays. I saw Gene one other time shortly before I left. He had brought me a cooling gel-filled mask – from the University. Unfortunately I had the nurses put in their freezer for me and I forgot it when I left.

Tracy – Wendy's

I had known Tracy since I was a co-op at Dow Corning back in 1989, and then again when I worked at HSC as an LPO in 1995. I would walk my rounds and stop to talk to her in the lab. I had a lot of schooling for my job and she and her family would look after my cat while I was away. Eventually she and her family took him in permanently because with my work schedule I was never home. Years later I started work at HSC again and she was in the lab that I hired into. Over the course of that first year she and I became fast friends. I would learn later that she was shocked when she initially saw me in the condition I was in at the hospital. She told me later that the first thought that went through her head was, "Holy shit!" She had not expected to see me like that. I had my arms and hands curled up and I almost slid out of my wheelchair because I could not sit up straight and hold myself in. She fed me three or four times when she came to visit – I don't remember these instances but I know they are true. One of the last visits, she brought me a bowl of chili from Wendy's. She said then she saw progress because I was able to hold my own spoon. It was clear to her that I was getting better. Sometimes when she came to visit I would be in PT and she would come down to watch me and we would spend time together.

□   Leigh/Marty – Jimmy John's

Leigh is my cousin and Marty is her husband. They live about two hours from me downstate. One day the nurse told me I had a visitor at the door and when I asked who it was, Leigh piped up and said, "It's your cousin…" I was so happy to see her and her husband and I was so surprised. I don't remember the last time I had seen them. They came to visit me a few times and one of the last times they were there they brought me an Italian sub from Jimmy John's (per my request). Once when they were coming to visit me, they called ahead. I had about 30 minutes before they got there. My caregiver for the day, Ebony, and a nurse on the floor jumped into action. They quickly washed and styled my hair, and dressed me so that I would look presentable. The nurse actually braided my hair. It was nice that the people on the floor were that considerate. And quick!

□   Cheryl – popcorn/pop

Cheryl is someone who I worked with at DC for a couple of years before she retired. Her husband had worked with my uncle – Leigh's father – in the educational system years prior to us working together. Cheryl would drop by every couple of weeks and bring me big bags of popcorn and 2 liter bottles of caffeine-free Diet Coke. She also fed me on occasion but I don't remember any of that.

□ Kay/Bill- Dunkin donuts/BK/Lettuce lounge/pizza

I had worked with Kay for many years before she retired. When I knew her at work, she had become a mentor of mine and it seemed only fitting that she and I would remain in contact after we both left the company. When I first started getting sick she came to my house and helped me write out some bills because I couldn't see very well. She is the one who initially sounded the alarm and said that I needed to get to the hospital. I told her I would, but that was an empty promise because I couldn't see to drive, and I wouldn't call an ambulance because I couldn't afford it. Kay and her husband Bill came to visit me in the VA and brought me food, sweets that I would never have eaten before I got sick. Kay was amused to see me eat not one, but two, donuts in one sitting. When Christmas time rolled around and I was able to choose gifts that were donated from area businesses, I made sure to get a few gifts for Kay's family.

□ Teri/Mitch

I knew Teri and Mitch from a church that I had attended in St. Charles with Tracy and her family.

I had helped out at various functions, helped clean the church on occasion, set up tables and do a lot of dishes after community dinner functions. They both came to visit me when the church had other business at the VA and Terry came back to see me once in February. In fact, she was there during my PT the day I stood on my own for the first time in four months.

□   Don – psychologist/friend/mentor

Don came to visit me to see how I was coping with my issues and to offer support. He's a friend of the family but I felt confident that our conversations would stay between us. He would later fly with me to my parent's house in Florida and help me to begin documenting my journey. He continues to be a great sounding board.

□   Keith- former patient

Keith had been a patient when I was admitted to the VA. He was loud and obnoxious in his own way, but he kind of grew on me. By the time he was able to leave I was sorry to see him go. He reminded me of the father on the TV show "Everybody Loves Raymond". He was able to leave the VA shortly before Christmas and he came back for a checkup. He stopped by my new and larger room because he wanted see how I was doing in it. It was nice that he made an effort to find me.

□ Doug/Sandy – patient leaving

Doug was also a patient when I was in the VA. I think I interacted mostly with him during occupational therapy. Sometimes fellow patients would be there at the same time and we got to chat with one another. When Doug was checking out he, and his wife Sandy, stopped by my room so that he could introduce us. During that visit he told me what an inspiration I had been to him. I thanked him for his feedback but I was thinking to myself, "What on earth could he be talking about?" They left me their address and phone number so that I could follow up with them after I was discharged. I wish they'd have left me an email address but to call them out of the blue just isn't my nature. I never did.

MIMI

<u>Meeting her</u>-The unique thing about Mimi and me was that we were a minority in the VA. Out of 33 beds, we were the only two that were female for the majority of my stay. She stopped by my room one day shortly after I arrived to say hello. The first thing I noticed was that her wheelchair was automated. Not only was mine not automated but I couldn't get it to move on my own. I don't remember what we talked about but it was probably what brought us to this place. She seemed like a really nice person. One of the caregivers had warned me that

Mimi wasn't exactly a positive person. I thought I understood, but when it came to Mimi, negative took on a whole different meaning. I would soon find out that she wasn't just negative but that she used that negativity to manipulate others. I guess I was lucky because she took a liking to me. If she hadn't, how boring my overall stay would have been. She had a sense of humor. Other times after dealing with her, I would just sit and think to myself, "You've got to be shitting me."

Lunch- it turned out that neither one of us really liked to eat at the cafeteria. For my part I hated to have other people watch me needing assistance. It's not that the people weren't nice, they were (After a while some of the characters I got to know, either on purpose, or through osmosis). The first day that Mimi and I met one another we both ended up in the cafeteria around the same time. I had assistance because, I could not move my wheelchair- partly because I could not feel my fingers and didn't want to get them stuck in the spokes. I was placed at a table with two people, the fourth seat was blocked by a partition. I didn't give much thought to where she was going to sit. I mean, she had not asked me to lunch. I heard her come in behind me and complain that there was no place for her to sit. When I looked around I noticed an entire table with only four people sitting there in regular chairs, and the rest of the table was empty. They were all women. I think they must have been visitors because it was a while before we had other female patients on the floor. In any event, she directed shame and guilt at the caregivers because there was no place for her and she went back to her room. I thought at the time she probably wanted me to sit with her but I was pretty new there and I was more concerned about being fed and getting back to my room.

Food- according to Mimi, she only ate pineapple and cottage cheese. She made a big deal about the fact that she and her dietitian went round and round because that was all she wanted to eat. I might have believed this had she not weighed at least 300 pounds. Once, when we were at bingo, the guy who roomed across the hall from me asked her if she would like to split a pizza with him that night and she agreed. I wondered to myself what kind of pizza is served with pineapple and cottage cheese, but I found out later it was the kind of pizza that came with extra pork. She confided in me later that although they split pizza he never ate it with her. She told me his doctors said he had to cut back on his pork intake because of his gout. That meant no more two sausage patties every morning, and no more extra pork on his pizza.

Once during the holiday season, she asked me to come over to her room and watch some Christmas movies. I thought that sounded like a good way to spend the afternoon. She had access to Netflix on her computer and we picked out maybe three movies to watch that were holiday themed. I took a single-serving size bag of popcorn and a big Twix candy bar. Her room had two beds, but the other bed couldn't be occupied because she'd had MRSA. I noticed she had two coffee cups and two packets of hot chocolate. I asked her where she could get the hot water and she said she'd just called one of the girls to come in and make the hot chocolate for us. I didn't think that was what they were there for, but I kept my mouth shut. Because I could hardly get my hand to my mouth without spilling things all over the place, we opened my bag of popcorn and emptied some of it into a cup that I could hold onto while I ate. I had taken the bag of popcorn to share with her but when she stuck her hand in the popcorn bag I realized she had just claimed that bag of popcorn. Then she helped herself to half of my Twix candy bar. She had some hard candy and she offered me some but I refused. After that I had friends bring me large bags of popcorn and I would squirrel them away, so that when she visited my room I didn't fear her claiming another bag of popcorn. Perhaps this wouldn't have been such an issue but I discovered she performed her own catheter insertion. Yuck. Sometimes you refuse to share because you don't know where the person's hands have been. I leave the rest unsaid... except for yuck.

One night they had a special dinner for hospitalized veterans. They used real cloth napkins, the good china, tablecloths, centerpieces for the tables and offered a choice between salad or coleslaw, steak or chicken, mashed potatoes and gravy, green beans and apple pie with ice cream for dessert. Mimi took one bite of steak, chewed it for at least 20 minutes, claimed it was too tough and wouldn't dispose of it – and took off back to her room leaving coleslaw, potatoes, gravy, apple pie and ice cream. They had kids from a local middle school serving us, live music, and raffled off numerous gifts that night. She told me later that was no big deal because at a different VA, they did that all the time. I can neither confirm nor deny this claim of hers.

<u>Singing</u> – Mimi apparently had a singing voice and to prove it she had her own karaoke machine, microphone and music. To hear her tell it, she had once belonged to a band. She and Pam, the VA recreational director, would get together and sing duets often taking requests from the audience. The audience

rarely consisted of more than four people, that included me, and the playlist was only what she (Mimi) had made available to us on the series of discs that she had so we couldn't call out music from Michael Jackson or Barbra Streisand. In fact, she got upset when we did it as a joke. One day a woman who had been recovering from some form of cancer was moved to our floor. She wanted to sing, she had heard that we had a karaoke device and system set up. I was there the day Pam suggested to Mimi that we move the karaoke machine downstairs to better accommodate Clare. Mimi initially would have no part of it, and I don't mean to say she wasn't interested, she flat out said "no" so I asked her point-blank, "Why wouldn't you support our fellow patient?" I kept after her until finally she said to me, "Drop it." I thought, "Like hell..." So we set up the karaoke machine downstairs near the nurse's station so everyone could participate. This wasn't a Make-A-Wish being granted, but it was something nice to do for someone who clearly wanted to sing, and I could think of no good reason why we shouldn't allow her to do that. Mimi finally relented but as the woman started singing Mimi sat across the room and rolled her eyes. The woman wasn't that good but that really wasn't the point. She finally got to sing, and who would deny her that? The night of the dinner Clare sat down next to me and I tried to engage her in conversation, but it didn't fly, and across the table from me Mimi kept mouthing the words, "Please don't sing, please don't sing." I couldn't believe the nerve of her.

<u>Bingo</u> – Mimi and I first started going together to bingo so that she could help me with my cards. I hesitated going for a long time because I didn't realize that the cards they used were designed for people who needed assistance (the cards have little windows that the player pulls down when the applicable number is called). If I won even $.50 I would say to Mimi, "Well, that covers my gas money." There were two guys in there that we ended up sitting next to often, one was Keith and the other one was Terry. Keith and Mimi would sit together and Terry and I would sit next to them. Terry was always winning and sometimes when I wasn't winning, which was most of the time, he would trade cards with me so that I would win. He was a nice guy, he even put my name on a football board and I won 10 coupons. He left the day before Christmas. I never got a chance to thank him or tell him that I always thought he could've been a country music singer. He just had that kind of voice. One day two guys in wheelchairs came to bingo and Mimi said something to the effect that they were looking for the girl in the wheelchair. She said that meant me and I said, "What about you?" And she replied, "This isn't a wheelchair."

And my response was, "Well, it's got wheels doesn't it???" I didn't realize what a "wondo" wheelchair she had and from that point on I always referred to it as the Nymbus 2000. I would joke with my PT folks that I wanted Nymbus 2000 and they always shook their heads at me. I didn't know much about bingo before I started with the group but I know now that people take that stuff seriously. And of course now I know people have found a way to scam that system too. One time Pam called out one of the usual suspects for cheating. The debate between the two of them went on for so long that I dubbed the exchange "bingo-gate."

Travel without her wheelchair -Mimi had issues when she would have to go to other sites for medical issues and she couldn't be transported in her Nymbus 2000. She would complain about how uncomfortable the other chair was and the discomfort on a long trip to the other hospitals. I realized it was uncomfortable. I think we probably all felt that way, and really none of us looked forward to the trip. But the real reason Mimi was upset about not being able to travel in her Nymbus 2000 was because she didn't have access to her stores of graham crackers... or the other cache of food she had hidden in her wheelchair that wasn't a wheelchair.

One of the funniest things, in my opinion, was when I would express my opinion about Mimi, caregivers, nurses, and even my therapists just gave me a look. I said to them, "You can't say anything, but I'm a patient, I get to say anything I like." Read on and you will get my point.

<u>Rude to caregivers</u>-Mimi had a habit of being rude to caregivers. Her biggest pet peeve that I heard about, other than the cottage cheese and pineapple, was when they would ask her birthdate prior to giving her medication. It was a safety net of sorts for the caregiver. Mimi give them hell saying things like "I've been here for a year and you still don't know that it's me?" It would be one thing if Mimi wanted to give them a ration of shit while she was alone with the caregiver, but to put someone on the spot like that in front of guests and other residents – not cool. Once when I was in her room watching TV one of the evening nurses walked in and said "Hello." I responded, Mimi did not. The caregiver told Mimi that she had brought a new style of absorbent pads for her to try out at night. I looked at Mimi, expecting a response and she had her nose in the air. Not one to be daunted, I turned to the caregiver as she was leaving the room and I said, "Thanks!!"

<u>Sense of entitlement</u>-– there was a fellow resident by named Ed. When I first met Ed, we

were in bingo. He helped me clear my boards a few times. I never saw him in the cafeteria, probably because I didn't go there very often, but he was always very nice to me when I did see him. One day, out of the blue, he showed up at the door to my room with a big bag of potato chips. He told me he had seen the chips and he thought I might enjoy them. At this point, I was tasked with gaining weight so I gladly accepted them. One of the things I tried hard to do on my own in the VA was to stay away from caffeine. My doctor's had told me for years that if I could do without it, I should. Wouldn't you know one day I went back to my room and found a miniature caffeine-free diet soda sitting on my table? Later that evening I was out in the hallway talking with Mimi and Ed asked me if I had found my present. I thanked him for it. As we were sitting there, Ed put his hand on my knee and told me what a wonderful person I was and that everyone liked me and thought I had a great personality. I thanked him for his compliment, even though on the inside I was thinking, "Huh?" Shortly after that he wheeled away to get his insulin shot before he could have dinner. Mimi took one look at me after he left and said, "I'm not one to be offended, but what am I, chopped liver?" Ed had caught me so off guard I had no response for her.

Ed had gotten in the habit of coming by to visit me on a regular basis. He was a lonely guy and he roamed the halls endlessly. He was in a wheelchair also and I thought he'd been there for longer than I had. He wasn't courting me, I guess it's kind of hard to tell, really, but in any event, his wife (who wasn't his wife because they got divorced) and I got along well. The divorce was because she would not be covered medically if she was married to him. So it's not like the man was courting me, he was just being friendly and having said that - just before Valentine's Day he brought me a box of chocolates. I didn't think much of it but Mimi did. We were in my room trying to get an app to work on my computer when Ed rolled up behind us to visit. Mimi had recently returned from a visit to the Detroit VA hospital and she said to me that she was out of money because she had used all of her bingo coupons at the Detroit VA. She had not wanted to put anything on a credit card which I said was a good idea. Then she said, while looking over her shoulder at Ed, "Well I don't have a sugar daddy who brings me potato chips, pop, and chocolates." Ed just kind of grinned and I thought to myself, "What a bitch." The next day Ed told me he was going to the VA store to get Mimi a box of chocolates like he had given me. I told him I thought that was nice. What I didn't say was I thought she was a manipulative bitch. I was in PT the next day and I heard that Mimi had received her box of chocolates and I asked how they knew that. They said she was seen in the hallway with Ed and her comment to him was, "Oh, you didn't have to do that." She later told me that she had accidentally dropped the box of chocolates on the floor and had not eaten any of them. I would have been more apt to believe just about anything, but not that. One time she was in my room when a caregiver came in with a water for me and a soda for himself. She looked at him and asked," Where's my soda?" In the end he gave her his soda pop. I couldn't believe it.

Eventually Ed took issue with his treatment at the VA and started acting out. A patient in the room next to his was obnoxious and apparently kept Ed awake all night. Ed found this patient the next morning, rolled up to him in his wheelchair, and said to him (in front of the nurse's station), "If you make a ruckus like you did last night I'm going to break your jaw." Ed came by my room more and more often, complaining that no one was helping him medically, complaining about the VA wanting to kick him out, telling me that the company he used to work for was going to have to pay him for pain and suffering for the last 20 some years due to an injury. The money was going to go to him. He threatened the staff with disappearing and said he'd roll himself outside and freeze to death and asked how was that going to look in the newspaper? From my room I could hear him yelling at the nurse's station. At one point, Mimi rolled up to Ed to try to console him while he was cussing out the nurses. I saw that and told one of my caregivers, "I have no intention of going over the edge, but if I do, don't let that woman anywhere near me." He refused to eat and ended up on another floor entirely. He kept going to bingo sometimes with a sponsor and eventually without. He started giving his coupons to Mimi and me and told us to spend them however we wanted because he wasn't going to buy anything from "that place". The coupons added up to close to $100. I wanted to give the coupons back to the system somehow and tried to figure out a way to have a pizza party, or something like that for the staff, even if it was the staff for bingo. Mimi wasn't keen on the idea. The last time I talked to her she was going in for an operation on her hip. She called me to say goodbye and to let me know that I should go down to the VA store, figure out what I wanted and let her know, so that when Ed had finally left the VA, she could purchase what I wanted and send it to me at my parents' house. I put my share of the coupons underneath the pillow in her room while she was away at the hospital and I didn't leave a forwarding address.

Room- for most of my stay at the VA I was down the hall from Mimi. I had a single room with my own bathroom because I couldn't get out of bed to get into a chair or into the bathroom so they had to put me in a harness, a Hoyer lift, to get me anywhere. Mimi, on the other hand, had one room with two beds and her own bathroom. By the time I met her she had everything packed in there after being there a year. A month before I was discharged from the VA, they were moving me to another room in a different hall. Mimi encouraged me to refuse to move. I was moved that evening and it took about 20 minutes without fanfare or any complaints. What good would it have done? I got a bigger room, and yes, I had to share my bathroom, but the woman who was on the other side had a toilet next to her bed. I think her visitors were the ones who used the bathroom, which of course was a no-no. Personally I can't stand the idea of sitting on a toilet somebody else has used, but honestly, didn't I have other things to worry about? I guess when it comes right down to it, regardless of the scope of our world, we have to choose our battles. What did I have to complain about? I was well fed, they showed concern about my dietary needs, I was exercised consistently with a lot of care shown for my rehabilitation. They never once missed my medications, they were very attentive to that end, they brought me fresh water and to the best of their ability, they attempted to meet my socialization needs. One thing to keep in mind is that most of the time the things they did for me, they did without my assistance. In the beginning I couldn't sit up, roll over, brush my teeth, bathe, or feed myself.

I did call Mimi one time from my parents' house in Florida. I had been there about two weeks and I wondered how she was doing. I got her voicemail and left a message. I heard through the grapevine that she finally got out of the VA but she wanted to get back in, almost the same day. After that I don't know what became of her.

- You've got to be shitting me!

o My last MRI.

My last MRI was scheduled for the morning of the worst snowstorm of the season. Those in the know said it was the worst winter in 75 years. My MRI was scheduled at a local hospital which was fortunate for me because all travel to the Ann Arbor or Detroit VA's was canceled that day. Since my illness I have issues with twitching. It's a problem for me to lie still in a tube for as long as it takes. As a result they were going to have to medicate me on site. The night before the MRI they came in to put a stint in my arm so the receiving hospital could just add medication the next morning. There was a problem getting the line into my right arm. It was the worst experience I'd had, and considering I once had 16 vials of blood taken at once, that's really saying something. They finally got the line into my left arm and when they wheeled me away I looked at the floor beneath where I had been and all I could think to myself was "blood borne pathogens". There was a noticeable amount of blood on the floor beneath my wheelchair.

Not only was the snowfall remarkable, but it was bone chilling as well. I just remember going from the warmth of the hospital, for a brief moment into the cold, and feeling my snot freeze as they put me in the ambulance for transfer. Due to the weather conditions that morning the hospital was short-staffed as everyone was calling in having been either snowed in or stuck in a snow bank. As a result when it came time to take me to the MRI machine there was no one available to take me. Eventually they got me there but I'm not quite sure how it happened. Prior to being taken to the MRI I had to get prepped and the standard question was, "Are you pregnant?" I responded that I didn't think so but they had to run a pregnancy test on me anyway. That meant I had to pee in a bed pan. They placed it beneath me and apparently it wasn't placed just right because I ended up mostly missing it. When they came in to tell me the situation I asked them if they had a least enough to do a pregnancy test. Thankfully, they did. Of course this meant that they had to change my sheets and get me cleaned up prior to my MRI.

Once they had me set up and ready to go into the MRI machine they discovered a hole in the tubing inserted into my nose to provide me air during the procedure. I remember them talking about it and one of them asked the other if they had another tube available. They didn't. I remember thinking to myself, you've got to be shitting me. Between the catastrophic snowstorm, the pregnancy – bedpan issue, and them having to "MacGyver" my airline, it had turned out to be quite the adventure.

The night of the suppository.

One night I hit my call button to I get some assistance toileting. This entailed being put in a Hoyer lift, moved midair to the bathroom, and placed over the toilet so I could do my business. That particular night it was just after midnight when I hit my call button. After I had done my business my caregiver came in and after checking my sample indicated that what I had really left behind resembled something more like rabbit turds. While I was in midair she probed my rectum and declared, "My God it's so packed in there I can hardly get my finger in!" She had gloves on but she hadn't trimmed her fingernails. A fellow nurse, Jenny, stopped by to see what the fuss was and she, the caregiver, loudly proclaimed the same to her. She was convinced it was so packed in there that they wouldn't be able to get a suppository in. She tried lube and kept telling me to push to which I responded, "I can't." Jenny asked me if I were on pain medication. I didn't think I was. So they went into the hall to talk to the med pass nurse, telling him about how packed my rectum was. I remember wondering how many other people needed to know. Eventually I was transported back to my bed and had to wait a good half hour before the 'suppository insertion team' showed back up. Once that happened they told me it would take about 30 minutes to take effect. I wasn't taking any chances so I didn't call them back for about an hour. Thankfully it worked and no enema was necessary.

In hindsight, it would have been faster to get a double cheese burger in me and let that take effect. After that night, if they asked me if I was feeling constipated I thought 'no fucking way- I am a lot of things- but constipated – I am not!', and then I would call for a cheeseburger from the non-patient cafeteria.

o   Hawaii

There was a fellow patient who I nicknamed Hawaii because he claimed to have a wife waiting for him in Hawaii who was going to give him an all over body massage when he got home. I suppose that's all well and good and the fact that he came across as a version of Santa Claus with an anger management problem shouldn't have turned me off at all. He would often wear a T-shirt one day and then wear it backwards the next day or inside out. He would wear his shoes on opposite feet which I can't think was comfortable in the least. Then one day, when I was in OT at the same time, he took a 3 ft. shoehorn and tried to swallow it, much like that of a circus sword swallower. One of the OT technicians saw him and loudly stated, "Get that out of your mouth."

o   Cop in a wheelchair

One of the patients I met in the hallway just outside my room was a police officer. He started a conversation by telling me how good he looked in uniform. He said that's what his wife first liked about him when they met. He went on to tell me about how much money she made and how they were going to move downstate. Apparently this was his second stint in the VA hospital due to alcoholism. He even showed me how much his hand shook. The conversation itself wasn't so remarkable it's what happened afterward it struck me as odd.

A day or two later I was in my OT with my usual OT technician and she told me that this same police officer had told her that he had given me his and his wife's phone number in case I needed help. I looked at her and I said, "He said what?" She repeated herself. I said to her, "I know you're not joking, because you don't joke." She agreed. I told her I had only ever met him once and there were no phone numbers exchanged. How odd.

Current reality and aftermath – Analects

"We cannot help but be fascinated by a situation we cannot imagine ourselves in."

- Food- what to eat next...who thinks of that?

If you've ever been unable to feed yourself it seems strange when you're faced with a plate full of food you didn't order and can't recognize. Sometimes the caregivers ask you to tell them if you want something to drink, and during the course of the meal, they'll ask you if they're giving too big bites. You would expect that. What struck me is when I sat with a plate full of food in front of me consisting of say, Turkey, mashed potatoes, peas, and cranberry sauce, or, a plate with a hot dog, baked beans, and a salad and they asked me what I wanted next. They weren't referring to the next meal or dessert, they meant what did I want from my plate next? That was strange to me. When you're actually feeding yourself you just do it (or some cases when it comes to peas, just don't do it). I remember asking the caregivers on occasion, "When you are feeding someone do you ever get sidetracked and accidentally take a bite yourself?" They always told me no, that's never happened, but I have to wonder if at any time they had a serving half way to their mouth and thought, "OOPS!"

- Hands burned to touch metal.

One of the most frustrating things, for me, about being bedridden was the fact I couldn't help anybody help me, physically, I mean. I could talk to them to tell them if I felt pain, which normally I didn't, I had no headaches or stomachaches. I had no pain in my arms or legs, but what I did experience was easy to feel, but hard to describe. I couldn't help them roll me over or sit me up when it came time to wash me, change my clothes, feed me, get me to the bathroom, or help me into a wheelchair. Once they had me on my side I would try to grab the bed rail to pull, or at least steady, myself so they could do whatever it was they needed to do. My hand holding on to the bed rail was like trying to hold onto a stick of butter, it seemed to go right through. Because I could not control that, I would throw my arm over the bed rail and hook my elbow there. Eventually I couldn't touch anything metal without my hands screaming with pain. To touch the cold metal sent me in orbit, I didn't know it then, but that was the onset of neuropathy. Regardless of how much better I get, this place in my life will never be forgotten or overlooked, because that constant reminder will always be with me. I decided when was still in the hospital that I if came out of this experience with neuropathy, I would gladly take it. If this is my lot in life, I accept it.

- What it's like to not be able to feel w/your hands…when you used to.

Trying to describe the feeling my hands, or the lack of feeling my hands, is odd because I have both. I liken it to wearing gloves, I also liken it to a sardine can where you can peel off the top layer of metal to get to what's inside. I can't peel off my skin. I take medication so that I can touch things without the feeling of a burning sensation. When I was first in the hospital and had a wheelchair I didn't even attempt to move it on my own because I had no strength. But when I was able to wear gloves so that my skin didn't touch the metal of the wheels, I had another problem – I didn't know where my fingers were in relation to the spokes on the wheelchair. I was afraid of having my fingers crushed. I think that was a very valid fear. In the end I wore gloves that looked like biker gloves and I would move the wheels using the palms of my hands. Once I got out of the hospital, and I was in my parents' home, I would try to increase the dexterity of my hands by putting pills in my pillbox for my weekly medications. I could brush my hair, brush my teeth and I picked up drinking glasses with two hands for the longest time. What became increasingly apparent was that, although I could see a brush to pick it up, it wasn't easy to grab what I couldn't see. When I grabbed my shirt to pull over my head I couldn't feel it with my hands, but I could feel the shirt moving past the hair on my head, and eventually saw the shirt in front of me after I took it off.

One other thing about not being able to feel my hands like normal was controlling the amount of pressure for opening a bottle of pop or holding a sandwich without squishing the stuff out of the other end. I could no longer cut my fingernails or toenails. The issue about the toenails wasn't just that I didn't know how much pressure to apply, but it was also that if I were to cut myself I probably would not feel it. I could very easily get an infection, which could cause untold damage, and the worst case, I suppose, would be death. "Wouldn't that be something," I thought "to come all this way to be felled by an infected toenail?"

- Controlling myself

In the beginning of my stay at the VA hospital every morning I would wake up at the foot of the bed. And countless times the caregivers would come in at night and put my legs back in bed because they were hanging over the side. I couldn't control the movements of my hands and legs, and as a result, I often found myself kicking or hitting the railings of my bed. They couldn't put up all four rails of my bed because that would be a security hazard (if I needed to get out of bed and fell while trying to climb over them). The semi-solution came in the form of body pillows. They had a pillow they placed between my left leg and the railing so that when I kicked it didn't hurt me. They had a second pillow that was shorter and they placed that between my right leg in the empty space where the railing would have been had they raised it. I nicknamed these pillows "Joe" and "Joe Jr.' I explained to my visitors that if I were to have men in my bed I wanted to know what their names were.

One of the strangest things, because I couldn't control the movements of my hands, was having someone else brush my teeth for me. I think I would've paid to have some dentures at that point- then I could have just popped them out.

Comments from Kay;

During my visit home Kay came by to visit me on July 18th and we had pizza. As we talked, she recalled visiting me in the VA and that when they first came to visit me I sat with my arms and hands curled up underneath my chin; my feet couldn't stay on the wheelchair supports and she kept putting my feet back on the supports because I couldn't feel them. At one point she told me, "I'm so glad that's over (my hospital stay), I mean, I'm sure you are too, but it was painful to see you that way."

Comments from Laurel;

Before this all began I was a full blown alcoholic, and as I type this, I am a full-blown recovering alcoholic. It is not something that I am going to apologize for, but it is something I need to own up to. In the months leading up to my illness my friend Laurel was very irritated with me. When we talked on July 18th, during my home visit, we were able to talk about what she was feeling leading up to our discussion the previous September before my illness became full blown. She said she had been frustrated with me because I wasn't taking care of myself and I acted as if I wasn't there, as if I was in a fog.

She couldn't get through to me and didn't know what to do, in part, because she believed it was a direct result of my abuse of alcohol. My hands shook; I had panic attacks; I had no appetite so I didn't eat. In hindsight she felt bad because she was my emergency contact and she wasn't there for me. She said she had been beating me up for things I couldn't control, things I wasn't even aware of. I told her not to worry about it, none of us knew I was being attacked by a virus in my brain. She reiterated that she felt bad that she had not been a good friend to me and that she did not deserve this friendship. She said that it was clear I had gotten over her lack of support, and that she needed to forgive herself. She had told me I could count on her and it became clear that I couldn't. And I knew it at the point of my descent.

• The scope of things –

When I was in college I took a criminal justice course in which the professor (my dad) explained, in real terms, what the scope of things really meant. He talked about the prisoner who wanted to write a letter but his pencil was dull and it infuriated him because he couldn't get a sharp pencil. You have to ask yourself what does a dull pencil really mean. In the big picture, probably not very much. But in the scope of his world it meant everything because it was all he really wanted. That's all he could really use. Years went by and my grandma lived next door to me. One day she called me up to tell me that there was a lone black bag sitting in the empty lot next to our duplex. She could see it right out of her kitchen window. She wanted me to move it, I didn't want to be bothered. I went over to her house and I tried to reason with her that it wasn't our lot, I had no business going over there and even touching the black bag, or even worse something hideous could be found in it. She replied, "Well then it needs to be found." She told me if I didn't go and pick up the bag that she would go and pick it up after she got home from playing cards. I was raised in a family that did not allow an 88-year-old grandmother to walk across an empty field, break her hip and fall down. On the other hand, the implied control drove me insane. I went home and called my dad and told him what was going on. He asked me if I remembered the lesson from college about the prisoner and the dull pencil. I did. Then he said, "You have to remember that is the scope of her world." I moved the bag. Fast-forward to my illness. I had been in the hospital probably two months, maybe less, when I asked for some ice for my hands because it seemed to be the only thing to ease the burning sensation. Up until then I had never complained of pain. Other than water and bathroom breaks I had not asked for much.

So I asked for an ice pack for my hands and they told me I couldn't have one because it wasn't in my orders. I was so upset. I remember thinking if I had asked for aspirin, which would've helped almost immediately, would they had made me wait? Not likely. But that was the scope of my world at that point and I remember thinking, "You have got to be shitting me."

Day of Discharge

As we drove away, the day I was discharged from the VA hospital, I imagined it dwindling in the rear view mirror along with all of the people I had met during my stay. To those I had befriended I wanted to say, "Please keep up with me" – not just stay in touch. I wasn't ready to become someone they used to know.

Even though I was apprehensive on some level about leaving, I knew it was time for me to move on. As I watched the cars drive along the street and pedestrians walk along the sidewalk I felt in that moment as if someone had pushed the "play" button on my life. Interestingly, I never noticed when the "pause" button had been pushed.

It was a remarkable feeling to be on my own again even though in reality it would be months before that would be true. It was remarkable because, in a sense, I could do anything I could imagine. I had not become "institutionalized" even after the four months I had spent there.

I promised myself to return there one day. I knew the one way to truly show my appreciation for their unshakable belief in me was to follow through and succeed. That way, perhaps, I wouldn't be someone they used to know.

Before my departure from the VA hospital in March 2014 a few notable things occurred.

On February 28 I had a visit from Dr. Oz – they called her doctor Z but I called her Dr. Oz after the TV show. It was my last night at bingo and Dr. Oz pulled up a piano bench beside me afterward and, we had what could only be called a lengthy follow up consultation about my stay at the VA. She surprised me by telling me how much she appreciated my upbeat attitude, lack of histrionics and willingness to cooperate with all of my caregivers. We talked about a lot that night but that was the take-away for me. That was the first time that anyone had ever commented on my attitude.

Sunday, March 2nd

I received a big Mennonite chocolate chip cookie from Katie. She was one of my caregivers and often did the med pass. She's the one I nicknamed Holly hobby, don't ask me why, but the name just fits.

That evening I also received moo goo gai pan from the Chinese Park Asia restaurant. My caregiver Bill provided that for me and I ate it while I watched the movie "Capt. America, the Original Avenger" in my room.

March 3rd

Tracy came to visit me and she brought me lunch consisting of "cuties" fruit and Wendy's chili. She also brought me two books, one on boundaries, and the other one was a devotional prayer book.

Dr. Don showed up and provided me with my flight itinerary and discussed the details of the upcoming trip. We were going together to Fort Myers, by way of Atlanta, to establish temporary residency for me with my parents.

March 4

In the morning, before he ended his shift, Bill came in and gave me a hug. He told me how much he felt I had progressed and that he was so proud of me. His parting comment, "Keep up the good work!"

Sandy, the PT person who helped me walk again, nicknamed Maytag by me because Sandy liked to agitate me, shook my hand and said, "I am really proud of you, you have come a long way, keep in touch." Then she handed me her business card. I teared up at the time because I was so moved. Her comment had special meaning to me because I held her in such high esteem. I had learned to trust her and always believed during my rehabilitation that she was never going to set me up to fail. She would not have let me. One might think that would be an obvious expectation, but if you've ever been through therapy, you know that's not always the case.

Pat and Ray came to pick up the remaining items that need to be taken to my home or mailed to my parents' house in Florida. As they were leaving Pat gave me a hug for the first time ever in the 14 years they had known me and told me that she loved me. She got dewy-eyed and expressed that she didn't believe she could have remained as positive as I had been through all of what I'd been through at that point. Ray said a prayer, wishing me continued recovery and he also gave me a book entitled "God's Promises".

Sue (Red Squirrel) and Judy, (Mrs. Garrett), came in my room to see me. Sue told me, "You are the best patient ever because you are always so positive – never yelling at us or kicking us out of your room – despite of what might have been a very difficult day for you."

Judy give me a hug. She was the one who tweezed my eyebrows and trimmed my fingernails. She said, "I am really going to miss you. You are so sweet." She was sniffling as she left the room.

March 5 departure day

Mickey, the janitor, came into my room and told me, "It was nice getting to know you". He shook my hand and wished me well. He's the one I could never convince to knock on the door before entering my room in the morning. I think he never got used to a female patient being around, or he's a randy old dude!

The lunch guy, who always called me Jo Ayres, brought my last VA lunch to my room. When he picked up the tray after I was finished eating he gave me a hug and wished me well.

Jeff, the recreation guy and weight trainer, came in to wish me well and said, "I like you, but if you ever end up in here again, I will kick your ass!".

Jane (supervisor OT) came in to visit me. She is the one who worked with me on my cooking goal. She had taken me off-site to the VA annex where they had a kitchen set up. Part of my recovery in OT was to be able to handle a sharp knife and make dinner. The day I was leaving she commended me on how far I'd come.

Pam Spencer, the recreational coordinator for the veterans on site, came to see me off and gave me multiple hugs.

Scott, my former Tae Kwon Do instructor, Vietnam vet and veteran advocate came to see me and made sure that I knew I should contact him when I got back home.

Janine was my caretaker that day and with about an hour to kill she gave me a shower and a hug goodbye. We also exchanged email addresses and phone numbers.

Mary, my OT person, came in for my last breakfast and we talked for quite a while. I told her that many people had commented on my attitude and progress. Mary was interested in my background – not about what had brought me to the hospital 4 months prior – she wanted to know what had shaped the core of my personality. I confided in her about my biological mother and her hatred of me. I never knew why, but I was certain she did. She told me she hated me when I was 10 years old. I went into specifics because she seemed to be interested in my story. This background moved Mary to tears and she said it made her sick to her stomach. I told Mary that she could share my background with Sandy it ever came up. Later that day, when I was in my last OT/PT session, Mary came to me and said that what I had told her was unfathomable to her.

Dr. Don and Tom Spain arrived after I had received my meds and was ready for discharge. Don and Tom loaded my bags into Tom's van preparing to head for the airport. As Pam Spencer wheeled me toward the exit of the hospital all of the caregivers at the nurse's station took turns bidding me farewell, each giving me a big hug. Mary was standing near the exit waiting to give me one final hug and told me that she was really going to miss me.

On to the airport...

Prior to hitting the road to the airport Tom stopped at a gas station to pick up a few items for the ride such as coffee, sodas and chips. I wasn't having a soda or any other kind of liquid. Even though I had practiced transfers with Mary and Sandy I was determined not to have to pee before I got to my parents' house later that evening. And I didn't!

I wrote this shortly after arriving to stay with my parents...

I had never anticipated seeing the world from the vantage point of a wheelchair; and really, who does? And since that was the case, one can only imagine how utterly unprepared I was for other people's treatment of me, the questions they asked, and subsequently, my ill prepared responses.

I would often leave interactions thinking to myself, "Wow...I didn't see that coming."

In the beginning it was tough for me to determine the level of response anticipated. Then I figured it out – polite questions from strangers deserved polite answers and not my life story. In my case I find that others in wheelchairs rarely ask what happened to me and I never ask what happened to them. I don't know why that is and, since we don't talk, I'm not likely to find out.

Friends of my parents- people in the gated community where they live- are genuinely concerned about my progress and they anticipate a more in depth response. This normally includes the latest development -how therapy is going, etc.

Closer friends and family encourage me to share more readily; I think because they know more about the extent of my journey. They are more inclined to ask about my rehab efforts and other personal accomplishments – like the first time I made my own breakfast. Sometimes I find I need to censor myself; for instance, do they really need to know that the first time I tried to wipe my ass during recovery I actually wiped the side of the toilet bowl because I couldn't see or feel what I was doing? Sure it's funny, but do they really need to know? Probably not.

I don't anticipate seeing the world from the vantage point of a wheelchair for the rest of my life and that gives me hope. I realize getting to the point where I can walk again isn't going to be easy; but I have been told that anything worthwhile isn't easy. I am blessed to have encouragement from several people.

After Care

Learning a new routine.

The day I was discharged from the VA I flew to Fort Myers, Fla. to stay with my parents while I rehabbed. Getting to the airport was easy enough because a friend of the family drove me there. On the way he stopped at a gas station to purchase a snack and something to drink and when he did, he left the van's side door open. It was subzero outside. I hoped that was not an omen.

It was the first time I had flown since my illness and I didn't know what to expect. I was confined to a wheelchair at that point and I couldn't stand on my own without support, and even with support, I couldn't stand for very long. Since this was the case, I felt getting through security might be an issue. As it turned out everything went well; the TSA employees were kind, helpful, and very thorough. My dad had arranged for a friend of the family to travel with me. Previously I had traveled a lot - in the military, for civilian work, and for personal reasons. Most of the time when I traveled I could fit all of my necessities into the two carry-on items allowed on the plane. It was something I prided myself on so I never had to deal with the hassles of checked luggage. I did this time as well- the difference being I couldn't carry them. That never dawned on me. I had all I could do to transfer from my wheelchair into my seat, and back again, on the plane. We had a layover in Atlanta and Don, my travel buddy, had to transfer all of the carry-on bags to our next flight. Miraculously, the boarding gate for our next flight was right across from us, and not in another terminal. He also brought at least six bags, plus his guitar and a carry-on. As a result, when we arrived at our destination in Fort Myers, we had to fit four adults, eight bags, a guitar, a walker, and a wheelchair into the car. None of us had known what to expect and the result was quite comical. My dad and Don sat in the back seat with a wheelchair and a walker across their laps and I sat in the front seat with a guitar propped between my knees. It looked so ridiculous that a woman stopped mid-way through the crosswalk and took a picture of us. What's even stranger is that my parent's had access to my Uncle's full- size truck.

None of us really knew what was in store for us. My initial goal upon arrival was to get into the local VA system. I needed to find a VA primary care physician (PCP) so that I could begin rehab. That did not work out as planned; it was supposed to take two and a half months to be assigned a PCP and I couldn't start rehab until that happened. Fortunately for me, a Dr. Wener had a cancellation and an opening to see me. That visit went well as I was able to be referred for both PT and OT evaluations, signed up for a women's health program, and also signed up for an optometry visit. During that initial doctor's appointment I realized the departure date in my head had just been moved out one month and I had only been in town 15 days. My initial goal was to leave Florida in three months' time. That's the thing about deadlines – the sound they make as they whiz by your head.

Most of the initial appointments happened relatively quickly considering I was in town on a temporary status. The PT and OT consults went well.

During my physical therapy (PT) consult – which was in late March – I did seven wheelchair 'sit-to-stands' in 30 seconds. I did four before they started timing me. They recommended me for aqua- therapy at that time. During my occupational therapy (OT) consult one of the things they had me do was reach above the sink to the top shelf, grab a cone, and place it in the cupboard below the sink. I did this 6 times alternating hands each time. I did not use my walker or my chair. The therapist said he believed I would achieve a full recovery.

My dad and I looked for a local rehab facility with a pool, based on the feedback we received from the consult. It took the better part of a month before the 'fee-based' PT was approved. I could have gone to the VA for rehab but they had no spot for me in their schedule. We had plenty to do while we waited. My parents live in a community where there are plenty of activities available to keep a person busy. They have pool parties; karaoke night; tennis, boating, golf and the list goes on. I received a new computer for my birthday with touch screen capabilities because my hands still were affected adversely by neuropathy. I also received a voice recognition program that I could talk into and it would type on the computer screen as I spoke. I received a transfer chair from the VA so that my parents would find it easier to get me in and out of the car as we traveled around town. When I received my transfer chair the gentleman came and showed us how to operate the chair, how to fold it up, how to adjust the brakes, and other little tricks that made use of the chair easier. I thought the logo on the back of the chair was nice because it indicated that it came from a veterans medical supply company and had a little flag on it. It was only intended for use if someone was pushing me along but I didn't know that. The first time my mom and I went to Costco she pushed her cart and I used my feet to pull myself along because the transfer chair has little wheels on it (compared to a regular wheelchair which has the big wheels every one associates with wheelchairs). So toward the end of this trip my mom had bought me a strawberry smoothie and as we headed to the exit my mom had to wait in line to have her receipt checked. I was taking my time following her, in no particular hurry, my feet were moving me along, "doink... doink... ...doink" when out of the blue a blonde woman walked up behind me and asked me if I wanted her to push me. Even as I said "no" I unconsciously started moving my feet faster, "doink, doink, doink, doink" holding my smoothie, looking around and heading toward the exit. The woman began to push me anyway and I indicated that I was with the woman in pink in line. Without a word she caught up to my mom and then walked around me. A man who was with her stepped up beside me and said, "God bless you." I thanked him as he walked away. In the back of my head I kept thinking, "I can't believe that just happened." How very kind.

I continued with the exercises provided to me during the PT consult; and my dad and I figured out a way for me to get in and out of the pool without busting my head (or his). We used a gait belt placed just under my shoulders so my dad could help me balance and catch me should I fall. In addition we put my shower chair on the side of the pool for me to use as a handle. I also used the hand railing of the pool steps to balance myself as I got into the pool. We did the reverse as I backed out of the pool.

Once we received the approval, it wasn't long before I started rehab. During the 1st PT visit I had to fill out paperwork. I had to note current abilities and identify skill levels. They had listed walking short/long distance, standing long/short time, running, etc. It was then that I saw it listed- hopping...really...?

The first question was 'what things do you have trouble with?' and the very next question was 'what do you want to work on the most?'

I said to my dad, "What was I thinking? Screw learning to walk....I want to learn how to hop!!!"

We got into the therapy area and I said to my dad, "I don't see anyone hopping..."

They provided me with a combination of land and pool exercises. It's one thing to have the tools but an entirely different thing to know how to use them efficiently. A friend of my parents had loaned me pool exercise equipment, and of course we had noodles, but until the PT people explained how we should be using the equipment, I was doing little more than not sliding backward with my home grown exercise program. I do give my dad and myself some credit because we knew that aqua therapy was good for me; we just needed it to be fine-tuned.

Taking a shower in the VA was a breeze compared to what my mom and I faced when it was time for my first shower in their house. A few years prior to this, my dad and mom had remodeled their bathroom to accommodate a disabled person thinking one of them might have to use it. The shower had glass enclosures and it was designed with the floor sloped so that water would run into the drain; the need for a lip of any sort was not needed. The opening to the shower was big enough for a wheelchair to get through and on one wall they had installed multiple showerheads; one stationary and one handheld. That was the good part. They didn't have any grab bars installed and the controls for the water were on the opposite wall from showerheads. The first time I wheeled my chair into the bathroom, I stripped and used my walker to get to the shower chair inside the shower. It took a little doing with a lot of help from my mom for the initial setup, but I was able to wash myself and my hair. I had difficulty sitting in the chair initially because I had no support to lean on as I sat down and the same went for standing up when I was done. The chair could easily move and cause big problems for me. The next time I showered, we had purchased shower shoes, liquid soap and turned the shower chair so that I could use the back to support myself as I sat down. I think the first time took us 45 minutes to an hour, but we quickly adapted, and within a week we had it down to 30 minutes. That included undressing, showering, and dressing. Eventually it got to the point where I could towel myself dry and dress myself with little or no help, although I still couldn't stand on my own. I continued to use the walker and wheelchair. I used to joke with my mom that she knew for certain that I didn't have any tattoos.

It took a few months but eventually I was able to shower in my own bathroom which had a tub in it. We placed the shower chair with the back toward the water spigots and my dad and uncle put a grab bar in for me. Using my walker, I was able to step backward into the tub and sit on the chair. I have to say it was nice to shower, dry myself and dress all on my own again.

While in rehab, I was getting better at balancing myself, strengthening my muscles, and continuing on the road to recovery. However the neuropathy in my hands and my feet continued to be an issue. I was adapting but it was still strange. I could grasp things I could see, a thing like a hairbrush, but I still had trouble grabbing my shirt and pulling it over my head when taking it off. Rather than feeling it with my hands I had to learn to feel it move on my shoulders. I still had trouble opening pop cans and bottles, milk containers, sealed bags of any kind, and turning lamp switches. Getting dressed was a challenge when it came to buttons, zippers and Velcro.

I walked my first few steps by myself, without the walker and without leaning on a counter or anything else, on Mother's Day. I called my mom into my room after I told her I had something to show her. When she came in we chatted for a minute and she asked me, "What did you want to show me?" I got up from my computer chair and walked towards her. I said, "You didn't get to see my baby steps so this will have to do, happy Mother's Day." Walking still did not come easy to me but that was a start.

Living with my parents wasn't difficult, it was just a fact of life. For obvious reasons, living in their home was not like living in mine. We were very sensitive to the fact that I would need my space and they would need theirs. Sometimes it was as simple as me hanging out in my room and leaving them to hang out elsewhere in the house. Some days I just wanted to sleep and they let me do that. Living with them wasn't bad-it was just constant, a necessity, a realization that I had nowhere else to go, but also, what a place to stay. My parents are fun, updated on current events, loving, supportive, and willing to do whatever it took to help me achieve independence and overall health. My dad went with me to every doctor's appointment, every physical therapy session, asked me daily if I had my exercises completed and encouraged me one hundred percent. My mom also supported me one hundred percent, but kindly took after the mom side of things. Things like helping me shower, helping me dress, blow drying my hair, outfitting me in clothes, shoes and make up. She cut my nails, arranged for my haircuts, made my bed every day and did my laundry. She focused in on my health when it came to what I ate, when I ate, and how much I ate.

From the beginning, I made sure I took my medication on time daily. I was responsible for getting my refills by phone and filling my weekly medication dispenser. That activity helped me regain some dexterity in my hands. In the beginning I had a toothpick ready in case I dropped medication between the sections of the dispenser holder.

As more time went by I was able to take over dressing myself, albeit slowly, getting my own meals, making my bed and applying my own makeup (no eye shadow). It was a slow process and it took a lot of patience.

My last PT appointment in Cape Coral was May 31st. They had taught me planks, bird dogs and a whole host of other exercises including water activities. I began to enter the pool at home using the railing and stepping sideways into the pool without any other assistance. I was able then to also walk out of the pool using the railing and pulling myself up steps, left leg first, to reach my walker which enabled me to get to the chair to sit down and dry off. I no longer needed the gait belt, my dad holding on to me, or my wheelchair waiting for me when I exited the pool. It was a far cry from when I needed two grown men to get me into and out of the pool.

My dad and I started utilizing the recreational center located in their community which consisted of a building with exercise equipment, including exercise mats, and had a room that had a railing/bar along one side. We started going to that center every day. I rode the bike for 11 minutes and utilized the mats for another 35 minutes. Then I upped my time on the bike gradually and started using the bar to help me balance as I walked repeatedly along the wall. The first time I walked for 20 minutes. Between that and the bike that day, I thought my legs were going to fall off.

Within a matter of weeks I was able to hold planks for 30- 40 seconds; start level I side planks; and walk along the wall without holding onto the bar (I was holding onto a cane however). At first we timed my walking at 20 minutes and then 27 minutes but we quickly started counting the lengths of the room. The first time was 11 and then 14 lengths. We estimated it was about 720 feet. During this time, I began to experiment walking with a cane more; not for support but as a tool for balance.

Much to our surprise (and delight) the VA authorized eight more PT sessions at the Cape Coral wellness facility. The sessions started up again on June 18th. The first day back, they started me walking on the treadmill at the slowest speed possible and they wedged a large rubber ball in the frame as a target for me to kick as I walked. I stayed on the treadmill eight minutes. This was the most sustained activity, aside from the stationary bike, that I had since my illness began.

The next day my dad and I went to our fitness facility and re-created the newest work-out that had been outlined. It included biking, walking on the treadmill while kicking the ball, tying a thera-band around my thighs for resistance as I side stepped the length of the workout room several times, and the usual floor exercises.

In late May my dad received another bill from Health Source, and it pushed my total healthcare tally to well over $20,000. I was more than a little distraught. I had already reached an agreement with St. Mary's to pay that bill $200 at a time. These other bills that kept coming in were from $200-$7,000 each. I knew I would get disability for a period of time but that would not cover my health bills. My dad suggested we contact a lawyer to help work with the debtors and the lawyer suggested I file for bankruptcy. I wasn't keen on the idea but what could I do? It occurred to me that I had gone from being gainfully employed with the same company for over 19 years to being unemployed, disabled and bankrupt in less than 2 years and I was only 44 years old.

In the meantime, the VA had outsourced my vision care and I was in the process of getting eyeglasses for the first time. I had been using "cheaters" for years. My parents and I were planning a trip back to Michigan for my dad's 55th high school reunion and to visit friends. Initially I was going to be dropped off at my home to see how well I did on my own and potentially stay. However, my PT came through and I would not be able to finish that until August. It seemed that I would not go home for good until September. My parents would have preferred that I stayed with them through the winter because winter had been so brutal the year before while I was hospitalized.

Learning all about walking – again.

Learning to walk with a cane was harder than I imagined. At this point I only used a wheelchair when I went to Costco's with my parents or if I knew I had a lot of time on my feet planned. When I first began using the wheelchair I felt, and I was, so unbelievably dependent on others. Even after I was able to transfer from my chair onto the toilet, from my chair into the car, from my chair to my walker, it did not diminish the fact that I was largely immobile. Eventually I became more mobile using my walker and I was able to get out of the house and into the car, bypassing the use of the chair. I was able to make it halfway around the circle where my parents live using the walker. I was able to get utensils from the kitchen and things to make my breakfast and lunch, as well as toiletries and the like because of the basket attached to the walker. It was bulky but it was so nice not to be in a chair. People still held the door for me and people still inquired after my health. People I didn't even know would ask me if it was my hip or my knee that I had issues with and were surprised when I would explain that it wasn't either, it was a virus to the brain, and yes I was learning how to walk, and no, it wasn't because I had any kind of surgery, got hit by a car, or tackled in a rugby match. Then the time came when I didn't want to use a walker anymore. I wanted to use a cane. I'm not sure exactly when I felt like that. I liken it to getting a haircut. I can go weeks without getting a haircut and then one day I wake up and I look in the mirror and I think "Hey, I need a haircut". That's how I felt about the walker. In June during my next VA PCP appointment, the doctor took me off five medications and said he was pleased with my progress. Then I asked the doctor to be issued a cane. I got a cane that day and I was given some direction on how to use it but I wasn't very good at it. I am not sure even now how one prepares to use a cane. It took me a long time to be adept enough that I didn't have to hold onto somebody's arm as I walked along. If I couldn't do that, why not use the walker? So I started out using the cane to help me balance and I realized that my left knee was still my weakest part. That did not come as much of a surprise since I had blown it out twice, once when I was 21 (in Tae Kwon Do class), and again at age 25 (it was Christmas eve while I was stationed in Turkey). I thought I would master the cane the way I had done with the wheelchair and the walker. A month after I started using it I went to visit my friends at the Saginaw VA. Sandy asked me to come back to see her before I left so she could provide me some tips on the use of the cane. She told me then that if I were going to walk for long distances, I would probably need a brace for my left knee. I did not master the use of the cane quickly enough and it frustrated me. I kept telling myself that recovery is a marathon, and not a sprint, but damn, did I want to sprint to the end. Instead I continued to have issues with my left knee. The muscles just weren't getting stronger, so I had to concentrate on isolating those muscles. I didn't want to continue to walk with my leg straight or my knee locked. I tended to pause when I would step with my right foot, and then my left foot, and then cane. Add to this I continuously looked down wherever I walked. I didn't see this as a problem but my mom did. Traditional therapy, I would later learn, would focus on looking up...but with me if I looked up, I didn't know where my feet were. Eventually during my second round of PT the therapist gave me some exercises that would focus on my quads and hopefully rebuild the knee/leg muscles and regain the strength I needed to walk fluidly with the cane. From time to time, in my own room or in the bathroom, I could hobble about without a cane. It seems the only time I was able to walk even remotely fluidly with the cane is when I wasn't tired or had not been sitting for more than 30 minutes at a time. When did that ever happen? So in physical therapy, I started practicing bending at the knee, because even at that point, I couldn't bend down or squat to get toilet paper or a hairdryer out from underneath the sink. Heaven forbid if I dropped a toothbrush, for multiple reasons.

During that June meeting with my VA doctor, he also scheduled me to speak by phone with the gynecologist who had conducted my yearly physical because I was bleeding, sort of like a period, every 2 to 3 weeks. Later the next week, as promised, my gynecologist called me and talked to me about my situation. Then she promptly scheduled me for a transvaginal ultrasound and a follow-up with another specialist in July and August respectively. (How is it we women can talk endlessly about mammograms but those trans-vaginal ultrasounds, where they put a 'hoop-a-joo' up in our stuff, misses the radar completely? Well, at least in my circle of friends it does. When I had the exam done in July I said to the technician that I hoped I wouldn't sneeze during the procedure or that 'hoop-a-joo' might come flying out of me as if I was shooting target practice.)

I saw my PT man on July 1st and he was very happy with my progress. He said he could tell that I had been working out and that I had been following their instructions. By this time I was up to one-minute planks. Considering that when I started I couldn't even do a plank, I was pretty happy with myself.

In anticipation of going home for a visit, I contacted my friends to let them know my schedule. I wasn't sure what to expect, hell, at that point I didn't even know if I would be able to walk. I didn't tell my friends that I used to work with because it was summertime and I knew they would be with their families.

My mom had a free Sunday and she asked me what I wanted to do. I thought about it for a minute and told her I wanted to go to the beach. We found a great parking spot-handicap parking will do that for you- and spent a few hours talking to each other, listening to the waves, feeling the wind on our skin, and watching the other beachgoers. It was a nice time and I hoped we could do it again.

- Our trip back to Michigan.

The original idea behind the trip was for my dad to attend his 55th high school reunion. Fortunately it was in Michigan and allowed for us to visit other friends who are living in Michigan during summer. I was going to be able to stay in my home unattended for four days. This was going to serve as a barometer to see how well I did on my own. I looked forward to it.

The preparation- We were scheduled to be gone for two weeks. I had to decide what I could take with us in the car to help me throughout the trip. I chose my cane and my transfer chair. My theory was I couldn't use a walker on the stairs, and apparently there were going to be lots of them, but if I had to go long distances – like a shopping trip or walk around the block – then my cane wouldn't be enough. It turns out I chose wisely.

The trip itself was going to consist of two 12-hour days on the road to begin with, so my dad and I decided to visit the library and check out some audio books. I used my cane at the library and I didn't realize how far I had to go until I started my trek. I had been gradually weaning myself from using my walker and this little jaunt made it clear to me that my stamina was nowhere near where it needed to be, but I made it without incident. While my dad was in the checkout line at the library, I made my way to the car on my own. Once I got there I caught the attention of a woman exiting her car next to me and she asked me if I needed any help. I thanked her and told her I was okay. She said that I looked like I was working really hard and I replied, "Thanks, I've come a long way."

We started out on Monday morning around 9:30 AM. Our goal had been to leave by 8 o'clock so we missed that deadline right off. I rode in the front seat most of that day and the trip was largely uneventful. I learned I needed to get out and stretch my legs at the second pit stop. I could barely walk because, at the first pit stop I didn't get out of the car. I never missed another one. The first night we stayed in Cleveland, Tennessee. I was so exhausted that first day; it amazes me still how tired one can feel just sitting in a car all day. The next morning I was supposed to receive a wakeup call at 7 AM but it never came so I jumped in the shower at about 7:10 AM. It was interesting because we had left my shower chair at home in Florida, which meant I had to maneuver getting in and out of the shower using my cane, and the one hand hold in the shower. One of the amenities they provided was shampoo. Once in the shower I hoped the screw top was actually a flip top so it would be easier for me to get at the shampoo. It wasn't, in fact, it had a seal that I had to deal with (one handedly) while the whole time water was running everywhere. With one hand on the hand-hold, and one hand dealing with the shampoo bottle, I managed well enough. As I was drying off I heard my dad knocking at the door. I yelled to him that I was okay but of course he couldn't hear me, and I thought to myself, "Of course, they sent the deaf guy to get me." It turned out that my room phone didn't work so none of phone calls were getting through. We were underway that morning without further incident. Although I did tell my dad I needed a new toothbrush since I had dropped mine on the hotel room floor. In the car my dad asked me how I liked the shower chair, which I thought was a joke because we had left mine in Florida. Playing along I told him I didn't have one and he replied, "But the hand holds were okay, right?" I told him I didn't know what he was talking about. It turned out that they had the Handicap room, not me. Let's just say not being able to walk, bend, climb, or have a lot of dexterity in my hands had its disadvantages, but I managed well enough. Since I had never been in a handicap room I really didn't know what I was missing. My dad claimed he didn't know and I joked with him about the time he and I travelled together, got separate rooms, and I accidentally got the presidential suite. That night he was at my door in record time to let me know I had the wrong room.

My parents had recently purchased a new car which presented me with a lot of opportunity to figure out all of the bells and whistles on the dashboard. One of the first things I realized, while I was trying to load the first audio book, was that their new 'whiz-bang' car only had capacity for one cd at a time. This really wasn't an issue for either of them since I was in charge of changing the disc – still, I liked to hassle my dad about his newest acquisition, it went something like this, "Dad, I love the new car with its GPS capability, sunroof, rear camera and the rest, but you do realize it only holds one cd at a time, right?" It even had the capability to tell the driver about weather alerts, road construction and/or traffic conditions well in advance. That came in handy on our two-day trip. So there we were, stuck in a three hour traffic jam, and all the read out would say was, "Accident." My parents switched drivers every three hours. We made about 3 miles, in three hours, when my mom turned around, looked at my dad, and said, "Okay, it's your turn to drive."

We made it to Plymouth, Michigan around 8 p.m. that night and stayed with some friends of my dad's. They would be attending the same high school reunion. Early the next morning we headed off to Saginaw, Michigan. While I was in Saginaw with my parents I needed to take care of my car and house insurance, meet with a lawyer for my impending bankruptcy case (and get a list of documentation I would need before filing) and visit the VA to say hello.

VA-I had made arrangements to visit my PT and OT therapists while I was in town. It was just over four months since I'd left the VA's care. I told them I would stop by around 130 PM. I was nervous about seeing them again. My mom dropped me off in front of the VA entrance at a little after 1 PM. She asked me why I was hesitant and I told her I didn't know if, other than my therapists, anybody would be there, remember me, or would want to see me. I asked her to give me a time when she would pick me up. She told me to call her when I was ready and I said it would probably be about five minutes so she should just drive around the block. I got out of the car with my cane and walked through the familiar doors into the hall leading to the PT area. I passed a few people, no one I knew, and made my way down to the PT office. As I rounded the corner into the office, Sandy was coming out of the office, and she looked at me with absolutely no recognition and asked me, "Can we help you?" I smiled and replied, "You sure can." Recognition dawned in her eyes then and she said, "Oh my God! I didn't recognize you Pam." And she walked up to me and gave me a great big hug of welcome. Amanda was there as well and said that she wondered if I was going to stop by that afternoon. Then Mary was there and I noticed she had her hair cut. I was so nervous but I was walking with the cane, and I wasn't wearing any flannel pants, I was wearing a bra, a nice shirt, make up and had my hair blow dried. I had made it; I had returned and I was as happy to see them as they were to see me. There was a lull in activity in the office at that point so they had me sit down and talk with them. Almost everyone who had worked with me in the PT/OT phase was there. I told them about the trip up with my parents, about the traffic jam, about the handicap room, and about the basket on my walker being a big hit. I told Mary people would stop and ask me where I got my basket. Then they joked that people would get sick just get into the VA to have a basket. Mary was only staying until 2 PM that day and she asked me if I wanted her to walk me down to the nurses station because she had told them that I would be in that day. As we walked away from the office I looked back and saw Sandy staring at me. I said to Mary, "She's staring at me." And Mary replied, "She's watching your gait." I knew I needed help with my gait and I was glad Sandy was ever-watchful for me. On the way to the nurses station Pam, the recreation mastermind, saw me and she was blown away by my appearance. And of course she asked about Don, whom I had not seen in months. I saw at least 20 people that day ranging from volunteers, receptionists, doctors and of course caregivers. I sat and talked with most of them for at least a little bit. Several of them whom I had been dealing with for the four months I was there simply did not recognize me. There were hugs all around, some tears, and utterly no lack of amazement. I waited for Mrs. Garrett to get out of a meeting before I left. She didn't recognize me when she saw me. I waited for Debbie to come on shift and she didn't recognize me either. After a bit, I went back to see Sandy and we talked about some different exercises I could use, and some other matters too. I heard that Mimi and Ed had both been discharged, only to try to get back in the same day they had been discharged. I was so glad I went to see 'my people' at the VA. I promised to come back again. The five minutes I thought I would spend lasted 2.5 hours.

My parents attended my dad's high school reunion and returned to pick me up and continue up north to visit more friends. The first stop was in Tawas. We spent a night there. I remember walking up the staircase to my room (lots of stairs) and sliding down them to get back to the bottom. It would be a little later before I figured out to back down the stairs. We went for a walk by the water that evening, so I was glad I had taken my transfer chair.

The next stop was Cheboygan. We visited some friends, the Kaisers, that my parents had met during their boating years. The next day I took a trip with their next door neighbor, Beverly, when she went into town for a doctor's appointment. We stopped for lunch at a Chinese buffet (first time I ever had peanut butter chicken....Yum!). Between the doctor's appointment and the restaurant, I was glad I had my transfer chair with me. Beverly and I always found a lot to talk about despite the fact she was 40 years older than me. She had a terrific sense of humor and an amazingly positive attitude. We women were all sitting around one evening when the subject of Beverly's new boyfriend came up. I said to her, "I just want to know one thing, has anyone talked to you about STD's?"

The morning we were leaving the Kaiser's, I tried to take a shower in their guest bathroom. I was undressed and in the shower when I realized I wasn't getting any water out of the shower head. I fiddled with it to no avail. I didn't want to towel my feet off, get dressed and hobble my way to the bathroom door to ask for help. I sat down and 'showered' in the tub. At that point rolling over in the tub, pushing myself up to my knees, and standing up, were the only issues. I think that took longer than my pseudo shower.

From Cheboygan we went to East Sparta, Ohio. We stayed with my mom's Aunt June, who, by the way, has the best set-up bathroom a handicapped person could ask for outside of their own home. We were able to visit with my mom's Uncle Paul as well and have dinner with him. I had wanted to visit the Amish country – and by visit I mean drive there, see the countryside, and stop at a cheese house to get Amish cheese and bologna. The day of the trip was beautiful and clear.

On the way back to Florida, we went by way of Savannah, Georgia. I had never been there before and looked forward to seeing the sights. The night we arrived we stayed in a low-budget motel. The phone in my parent's room didn't work until I realized their phone was probably put upside down in the cradle as I discovered mine was. The next morning we coordinated our departure from the motel and took an open air trolley tour around Savannah. There was more to see and do but I was limited in mobility, so I was just happy to be able to say, "Been there, done that!"

The rest of the ride home was uneventful and we arrived back in Florida without incident.

- Medical issues persist

On July 10th I'd had an ultrasound to check out my uterus. They were trying to figure out why I was bleeding when I had not had a period in two years. I had been scheduled to see my gynecologist on August 7th after I returned from vacation. I looked up on the Internet to see what was wrong with me. I decided I had four options- I could have a hysterectomy, I could do the wait-and-see method, I could take medication so they (the cysts) dried-up like raisins, or I suppose they could have been removed. Most of my life I hadn't used much medication, and never had a major surgery, so I was all for the wait-and-see method. So I went to see this doctor I'd never seen before and we discussed my chart. He was amazed that I was on few medications given my age. He said he needed to examine me and he agreed with the wait-and-see method and recommended that I get a future ultrasound to see if anything had changed in my cysts. I was happy to agree with that, the pelvic exam part of it, and mostly the part where I didn't have to come back for almost a year. During the exam I told the nurse that I had a high startle response, so regardless of what he told me he was going to be doing, I would probably still jump. As he began the exam he asked me how I came to be in the situation I was in. I described my initial symptoms and resulting hospitalization. I told him they didn't know what really happened me but that I was getting better. I was exercising daily and taking my medications. At one point he told me he was going to insert the speculum. He warned me that it would be cold and I replied, "Not for long." He chuckled and said he had not heard that before. He completed the pelvic exam and as he left the nurse helped me get dressed and we talked about exercise. She was amazed that the symptoms hadn't led to anything substantial but she said that she was proud of me for continuing to exercise and getting healthy. She told me to get better and to continue to have a good attitude. She said, "In the end, you'll only have yourself being responsible for you." I agreed as I told her it's a marathon not a sprint. She told me to keep up the good work and I said I would. Soon after that the doctor knocked on the door, opened it up, and asked me, "Are you decent?" And I replied, "Of course I'm decent! What kind of question is that to ask women anyway?" He said they should keep me around to add levity to the place. I was happy with the visit and, no offense to them, but I hoped never to see them again.

- Learning how far I had come.

I had about a month ago before I left my parents' care when my mom and I went shopping for new shorts because my shorts were not fitting me correctly, I had lost some weight. The first time my mom and I had gone shopping after I arrived we were looking for bras and bathing suits. I was in a wheelchair shopping for the first time. It was difficult getting through the rows, finding the appropriate sizes and then realizing too late that we should have used the handicapped changing room. So there we were, my mom and I, struggling to try on new bras. I couldn't reach behind my back to fasten them and we had tried find some bras that fastened in the front with no luck. That day, trying on bathing suits was difficult because I couldn't unbutton or unzip my pants and when I stood up I had to hold onto something, my mom or the wall, to step out of my pants, step into the suit, stand up again to get the bathing suit over the top of me. It wasn't until the month before I left, when my mom and I went shopping again that I realized how far I'd come. I guess I didn't realize how handicapped I had been until I had the opportunity to try again. This time I walked in the store with a cane, I grabbed a cart that would function as a walker, I helped determine the sizes I thought I'd need, the colors of the shorts I wanted to try on, and I managed to choose the handicapped changing room. Once inside I was able to unbutton and unzip my pants, take off my shoes, stand up to try on new shorts, and turn around to see how they looked in the mirror. I still couldn't feel my hands as I could before my illness, but I had come so far and I was grinning like a fool.

Again, with about a month left my mom said to me, after a workout, that I should get into my bathing suit. I thought it was a great idea. I'm not sure why but it been a couple of months since I had used the pool. I undressed myself, put the two-piece bathing suit on, and used my cane to walk out to the pool. I was unsupervised and I didn't have my walker with me. I had to give up my cane in order to grab the hand railing to get into the pool. I found a place to hang my cane next to the pool, grabbed hold of the hand railing, and carefully sidestepped my way down the steps into the water. I sat down and realized I didn't have my flotation device. I wasn't sure that I could swim on my own so I stayed in the shallow end. Once my mom came out, she threw me my flotation noodle. I was able to put it behind my back and under my arms. It was the first time I had that much flexibility. Again, I was grinning like a fool. I thought back to the first few times I had gotten into the pool after I arrived in March. Among other things it had taken my dad and a friend of his, to get me into the pool. What you don't see in that statement is that they had to get me into the pool without my help.

My PT was coming to an end on August 21ˢᵗ. He had me ride the bike and then some other practices. Dominic told me about the hazards of sliding backward if I didn't continue my exercises. He taught me how to tweak my planks by spreading my legs apart, and for my side planks, to lift my arm in the air and do leg lifts 10 times. And, for my bird dogs, to add cuff weights to my hands and feet and to put a pillow underneath one of my knees so that I had to really work on my balance.

- Ku-ku trolley

One night, shortly before I left, my parents' the community had an outing on an open-air trolley. Basically it was barhopping, appetizers, and some live music and dancing thrown in for good measure. Fortunately for me, they had an extra step, so I didn't have to raise my left foot to my right knee in order to get up and on the trolley. Once on board and underway, one of the attendees started handing out shots. My mom and her friend Dale each received one and my mom stunned me by sipping hers. I can only imagine what she was like in college. I told her that was no way to do a shot after she complained about it being too sweet or too bitter. Seriously?

It was a beautiful night and at every stop I had plenty of people there to help me on and off of the trolley. When I exited the trolley, I would back down the stairs because I was afraid of pitching forward. After observing this one woman walked up to me and said, "I can tell you are used to boating." I chuckled, I had not thought about it, but she was right.

I was the youngest one on the trolley by far, and it was interesting to see the elderly on a party trolley doing shots and waving party favors at passerby, but it was one of the most entertaining evenings of my entire stay.

- What I am capable of vs. what I used to do.

The last day of PT at the wellness center I asked for a copy of my PT progress notes. I had never seen progress notes before so I don't know quite what I was expecting. They were helpful in a way that I hadn't anticipated, and not helpful in a way that I thought they would be, so I guess it was a draw. What I had thought I would find were notes on my weekly activities and perhaps that's what were in the notes, but they were so coded that I couldn't read them. On the other hand, what I did find was a record of what my issues were when I first started PT with them. I read about my deficiencies, my inabilities, and the potential for improvement. I found it more interesting that they listed capabilities that I had before I got sick. To see it in black and white that I was able to walk 3 miles a day, able to lift and carry 50 pounds, able to be active in Tae Kwon Do, etc. really struck home, because had I looked at that when I first began rehabilitation, I would have realized what a struggle I was facing and I don't know how that would have affected me. I am pretty sure that if I had not concentrated on 'look at how far I've come' instead of 'look at how much I have lost' it would have been daunting. It was never my idea not to dwell on what I couldn't do. I take no credit for that. It just never occurred to me to, and as I get healthier, I now make a conscious effort not to think about the fact that I used to walk 6 miles at a time, cook meals, or climb stairs without using my hands. If I'm disappointed about anything, it's that I walk so slow...and that I can no longer type over a hundred words a minute.

- The long goodbye

I knew 40 days before I was going to leave my parents care. The days and weeks kept rolling by, one by one, not really distinguishable from the rest. When the final two weeks arrived, I knew it was time to clean out my papers and decide what to take with me. My mom had scheduled my last haircut, and we discussed having a girl's day out with my aunt before I left. I didn't miss a day of exercise during those two weeks, although we had broken it down at that point so that I worked on the machines for an hour and I worked on the floor exercises for an hour. I alternated my workout daily, always beginning with 20 minutes on the bike. We talked about having a grocery list made out before I got home, we talked about the exercises I would do, the equipment that I would buy, and the resources I would need to succeed on my own. I knew I still had access to the Saginaw VA when I got home and I knew I had to get a primary care physician there assigned to me. I had to ask for continued physical therapy and request home care if it were available to me.

My parent's friends, people that I had come to know within the past six months, began to wish me well about a week and a half before I left. They congratulated me on how far I'd come, wished me well, and hoped to see me again. Soon. For my own part it was strange. I was so looking forward to going home, yet I had no idea what was waiting for me. I knew I had the bankruptcy case to deal with, I knew I had a lot of work waiting for me at home because when I had visited in July, I was amazed at how much paperwork had accumulated. In a way it was as if I had come back from the dead and had the opportunity to clear out what I had not used in 10 months. I didn't know if I'd get my cat back. I wanted to but I didn't know if I was going to be capable of caring for her.

Exactly one week before I left, my friend who was scheduled to pick me up texted me to confirm my schedule. Leaving was real. I had left my parents over the years and now I was certainly capable but leaving was not without trepidation.

- To have a party or not – to say goodbye or not...

The Friday before I was supposed to leave my mom asked me if I wanted to have a going-away party. My natural tendency is to fly under the radar but that wasn't the issue, not this time anyway, the truth is I felt I'd be too emotional. In the end I settled for just short of ducking out the door. My mom told me later that all of their friends had wanted to come over to wish me well. I explained to my mom that I thought I'd be crying the whole time and she replied, "What's wrong with that?"

Trip back to Walmart – Alone

My first trip back to Walmart was good for me because I was learning how to do it on my own without help from any of my friends. The first issue I faced was where to park. One would think handicap parking would be the best spot. However, because my balance was bad I needed a cart to walk behind more than I needed a close parking spot. I realized this when I noticed that all of the handicapped spots were taken. I ended up parking next to the cart corral. Before I had driven to Walmart that morning, I had stopped at Taco Bell and gotten some breakfast. I decided to eat it while I was sitting in the parking lot before I went into Walmart. I was hungry, but it turned out the food wasn't so great, so I only ate about half of it. I decided to put the remainder of it in my purse and take it with me so I could throw it away at the entrance of the store. I have to think of these things now because I can't just jump out of my car when I get home and carry it in to throw it away. When I got to the entrance of the store, my attention was occupied by some people standing in the middle of the doorway. I ended up waiting behind them. As a result I was halfway down the first aisle when I looked into my purse and realized I still had a half-eaten breakfast in there. So now I had to find a trash container without retracing my steps. I knew I was not in top form, so I couldn't just wander around the store. I had to know what I was going after, get it, and get the hell out. Since my illness, I find I tire so easily. I remembered my last trip to Walmart by myself when I almost didn't make it out the door on my own. As a result, I was happy to see a trash bin not far from where I needed to go. I went around the corner of one of the last aisles I wanted to get to, the one with chips, snacks, and refreshments, but as I went around the corner, I was blocked by a worker moving a pallet of pop. I was concerned that the shopper on the other side was waiting for me to pass through the gap. As a result I concentrated more on my ability to walk than I did on picking up the item I wanted. At some point, a stranger helped me get something from the bottom shelf and then I found myself retracing my steps because I had missed what I wanted in the snack aisle. I grabbed a can of cheese, put it in my cart. It instantly rolled out and hit the ground at my feet. There was no way I was going to squat down or bend over to pick it up, so I nonchalantly kicked it under the nearest display and grabbed another one from the shelf.

By the time I was done shopping - I had only gone down the food aisles- the woman at the checkout said she was going to come to my house because I had the good stuff.

I don't know how long I spent in the store that day, but I do remember a real sense of accomplishment.

When I made it to my car in the parking lot I took a minute to figure out how to load my groceries. As I stood there a woman nearby asked me if I wanted some help. I don't know what surprised me more, her offer, or my response. "Yes," I replied, "I would like some help."

Handicapizing my home and life

Being handicapped in my home took weeks to get used to. I wasn't prepared for the situations that I would find myself in or for the solutions that would work for me. There was only one way to find out – dive in. Because of the neuropathy my balance was dreadful and my ability to hold onto small things like lamp switches, coins, toothpaste caps, and even bottle caps were my initial difficulties when I returned home. The solution came by way of one of those little grippy mats that you can put in your drawers keep stuff from sliding around. A caregiver of mine, Judy, had cut one of these mats into fourths and gave them to me to take when I left. I now have those grippy mats strategically placed about my house – in the living room, bathroom, and kitchen. She clearly knew I would need something like that. I can't thank her enough for her thoughtfulness.

Operating in my kitchen was difficult because I couldn't stand for very long and because I couldn't really bend over to get into my fridge, without risking a fall. That meant that the two liters of soda pop that I bought could not be put in the fridge. When I walked into the kitchen from the garage with a package, I didn't want to set it on the ground because I couldn't pick up and I couldn't put it on my kitchen table because it was too far from my door. My solution, temporarily at least, was to put kitchen chairs strategically in my kitchen. One at the garage door and one next to my refrigerator. The chair at the door is just the right height for me to set things on and the one next to the refrigerator allows me to sit down as I dig through the fridge. Eventually I'd like to get a stool to put in my kitchen because it is a galley-style kitchen and it would facilitate my use of the countertops for cutting and eating my food. I found it difficult to get my food to my table or to the living room because I had to work with the cane. I used T-shirt bags to transport food, pop, and other small items. I still could not carry a plate. Next to my front door, I put a table so that when people come to drop stuff off, say the pizza guy/gal, they can just set it there.

Managing in my bathroom was also challenging for some of the same reasons. It took me a month to figure out how to shave my armpits comfortably. I couldn't stand at the countertop and lean against it, and I couldn't sit in my bathtub because getting in and out of it was an issue in and of itself. So I decided I could sit on the toilet since there was a counter beside it and access to towels – damp and dry- near by.

The first time I took my car out to drive I had to go to my lawyer's office. I realized that I missed my car. I was sitting in it thinking myself "I wonder what the temperature is outside?" I looked down at my dashboard, and lo and behold, there was the temperature. I also learned that one-way streets were my friends because I only had to concentrate on one direction of traffic flow. I have learned that drive-through windows are my friends and that if I want food in a restaurant where I have to carry it for myself as in a buffet, I can't go there. I can't eat inside at McDonald's, Burger King, KFC, or Taco Bell. I will never eat a salad bar again on my own and I love salad bars. I have learned the handicap parking isn't about being closest to the door; it's about where the ramp is located even if it's around the building from the front door of the restaurant. I have learned where to go to get drive-through pop in 2-liters. When I get fast food through the drive-through, I have to get it without the drink because I have no way to carry the drink in the house when I get home.

I have no idea how I'm going to get gas for the first-time. I can't pay at the pump because I had to file for bankruptcy and I have no credit cards. I have learned that I pay my bills online because the effort it takes going in to get stamps takes forever. Trying to write legible checks is a nightmare.

Back to the bathroom, speaking of planning ahead, it takes a lot of planning ahead just to clean the toilet. I have to put the toilet brush in a place so that if I fall I don't impale myself. I have to be able to get the cleaning liquid container open, I have to balance myself so I don't fall over while I'm standing over the toilet cleaning it.

I haven't made it down the basement yet, I needed someone to go there and get my detergent for my laundry and put in the back of my car, so that I can get it out when I get to the laundromat.

I even depend on the kindness of my friends to come over and take my trash out. The other day I dropped my trash bag in my garage and it fell between my snow blower and the wall. There was no way I could get that out of there. My friend Kay and her husband stopped over to un-wedge it.

I never anticipated how nice other people would treat me in the situation I am in. There is kindness in strangers. It isn't that I don't know evil exists, I do, I am not naïve, but that isn't what this is about. I had been home a month and a half and I finally needed take my laundry in to have it done for me. I went to the place on Center that I had always gone to have my laundry done. I pulled up in front of the laundromat and as I got out I expected to go in and get a cart to take to my car. The woman there, named Donnie, opened the door for me and asked me what I needed. When I told her she offered to get my laundry and soap from the car. I took my own soap because it would cost less per load. I already had my detergent paid for, so why not take it? She recognized me from before and asked me what had happened to me. I gave her a synopsis and she was so very kind. She told me to call ahead and they would bring my laundry out for me. In fact, in the future, she said they would come and get my laundry from me if I just called to let them know I was there.

I was so amazed by this, it just about brought me to tears. I had done this on my own, filled my laundry bag while in my wheelchair in my spare room, dragged it out to my car, and drove there on my own. I know I probably could have gotten help, but I kept telling myself, if I can't do this on my own – then what? I have more important things that I need to count on others for.

I am sure that my neighbors would've helped me – but that I did this on my own was one more sign of independence – an independence I crave so desperately since my illness.

The day before, I had loaded up my bag of trash from the house and put it on the back seat of my car, so that I could back down and put it out for pick-up the next day. I kept thinking to myself, "I can do this. And if I can't what then?" I was able to meet my neighbor across the street, Cindy, when I came home from dropping off my laundry. I was driving on the wrong side of the street to pick up my mail so no one had to do that for me. We were happy to see one another. I hadn't seen her in months, not since my time in the hospital. She called me once or twice when I was in Florida and tried to connect with me when I was in Michigan in July. I felt terrible about the fact she probably thought I blew her off but that wasn't the case. She just never seems to be home. Since I'd been home, I kept my blinds closed because I don't want someone just stopping by. I may not have showered for a few days, or I may be sitting on my couch in my underwear eating Cheetos. And really, who wants to see that?

Cindy and I chatted about 40 minutes about my progress, about her life – she had recently lost her husband – and at times she gets depressed. I don't know anything about married life, but I know about depression. So we agreed to go to a movie, a comedy, on Wednesday that week. I told her I probably needed to go with my wheelchair and that I knew the ins and outs of going with a wheelchair, being handicapped, and getting a handicapped space. She seemed very happy to know that I was okay and she said that was nice to see the light on in my window from across the street – just to know I was home. She also said that she didn't know me very well, but she could tell I was stubborn – and if I hadn't been I probably wouldn't be here.

Tracy came see me on October 20th – it was a one-year anniversary from when they took me to ambulatory care, thinking I'd be home 4.5 hours only to get home 10.5 months later. 4.5 in the VA hospital and six months with my parents.

In any event, I asked Tracy to come over to help me put down the window in my front door, open the toilet bowl liquid I had so I could clean, take my detergent from my basement to my car, move a table from my front room next to my front door, and slice some cheese that I had bought when I first got home.

Tracy didn't just show up to help me out with those five things – which she had told me were doable about a week before. She scrubbed my toilet with Pine-Sol, using a glove, and a rag. She scrubbed the whole damn thing. She scrubbed my bathtub, my bathroom sink, and cleaned my bathroom floor, my kitchen floor, dusted my house, vacuumed my house, cleaned my bathroom mirror, and wiped down everything on my vanity after she encouraged me to toss most of the stuff out. Of course she was correct – they were centuries-old.... at least to me.

Jo Ayres

Decision making

Since I've been on my own, I have found that each task I face can be categorized into three areas, namely:

1. Enabled tasks: easy solutions that are within my grasp such as using the TV remote.
2. Difficult Tasks: in these cases I believe that, with some thought, I can probably accomplish the task. It may take some ingenuity on my part but essentially I can accomplish this task if I am willing to invest the energy. For example, I can figure out how to take out my own garbage if I decide to do so.
3. Non-enabled tasks: these are tasks that I cannot or should not do on my own, either because I can't physically handle it.(For example: I am not physically capable of changing the smoke detector in the hallway.) or, the task would put me in harm's way. (For example, if I boil water to make spaghetti and try to turn around and dump the pot of water into the sink, I could easily spill the water and burn myself.)

The non-enabled situations call for help from my friends or caregivers. They fall into two categories, namely:

1. What I need. For example, I "need" someone else to change my smoke detector. Need = safety.
2. What I want. For example, I "want" someone to change the light bulbs in my garage. Want = convenience.

A 'want' is a challenge that I am reluctant to call on my friends for help. I am more apt to wait until either someone offers (possibly prompted by my hints) or when I can trap them when they visit.

I have also noticed that I as I become more skilled with living on my own, difficult behaviors can become enabled behaviors with consistent practice. I have to accept my limitations and realize that there are some things that I will never be able to do on my own. This realization has given me a greater appreciation for the role of friends in my life.

Holding on to my quarters

I filed for bankruptcy in September, 2014, due to my extensive medical bills. I ended up filing Chapter 13 because I had too much money in the bank to file Chapter 7 but not enough money to satisfy my creditors. In order to file Chapter 7 my bank account would have to have been down to $2000. I couldn't afford to do that because I still needed to pay insurance for my home, car and also the mortgage for my house. I ended up paying an extra $5500 toward my mortgage to get it out of my bank account. I couldn't put it into a Roth IRA (which would have been protected from the creditors because it would've been seen as retirement savings) since it wasn't earned income from that year.

The morning of the hearing was October 16, 2014. I had my friend John drive me to Bay City for a couple of reasons, one was I didn't know if I could drive that far, given the neuropathy in my feet. And two, I didn't really know where I was going in town. Through this whole thing, I've always felt like filing for bankruptcy was the most embarrassing. I thought "How could this happen to me?" I have been really good about saving money my whole life. I've always paid my credit cards in full before their due date. In my credit report, which spans 10 years, the only mark on it was that I was late for a payment once. I couldn't help but ask myself how I could have avoided this. But as John and I talked that day, he said to me, "If your illness hadn't happened, you wouldn't be in this situation." He was right.

I used my transfer chair to get into the building where the bankruptcy hearing was because the boots I wore at the time had a bit of a heel and walking with a cane kept turning my right ankle. I wasn't looking for sympathy, I was trying to make sure I didn't fall over.

We were there plenty early and as I sat in the waiting room I realized I had no idea what was going to happen next, not in the next hour, the next day, week or month. I guess I wasn't any different than anybody else at that point. Who really knows anyway? I went into the hearing room on time and I was surprised at how many cases were there ahead of me. Thursday is apparently when they hear Chapter 13 cases which means we were all there for the same reason. There was a table in the front of the room where the trustee, creditors, and lawyers sat. When people such as me had our turn, we moved to that table as well. In the back of the room there were rows of chairs where those waiting to be heard sat and waited their turn. When you go up to the table, the trustee introduces himself and then goes through a series of questions, checks your ID and your Social Security card. He asks if that's really your signature on the filing. You state your name and address for the record. If there are any creditors present they have the opportunity to ask you questions about your filing at that time. There was one creditor present who seemed to represent every credit card or credit union in the local area. He asked all kinds of questions to the various applicants and I thought to myself, "What a shitty job". I felt bad for the applicants who were questioned. The whole process is embarrassing, stating your name in front of a group of people you don't know, and then being quizzed by a creditor who has no idea what your history is or what made you come to this last-chance situation. I was fortunate there were no creditors there to ask me anything. On the other hand, the trustee knew who my father was and revealed that his father and my father used to dock their boats across from one another and had plenty of good times together with a couple of 'pops' on the back deck of my dad's boat. He asked me about my mom; he knew her name and her profession before she retired, he asked me where they were now, whatever happened to the boat and things of that nature. I have no idea what the people in the in the audience thought. The look on my lawyer's face was priceless. He knew that my dad had been a figure in the community but I don't think he had a clue that the trustee's father and my father were good friends. As I told a friend of mine later, on one hand, it was embarrassing, but on the other hand, it was really comical.

After you to state your name and address for the record, they ask for any creditors present, and then they ask the lawyer if he has any questions. They talk about garnishment of your wages, or in my case my checking account, how much money would be paid monthly, and for how many months. Figuring this means the entire room is able to hear how much you owe and for how long you are going to owe it. I know that my ruling was for a fraction of what I owed, so that means when I heard people were to pay a thousand dollars a month for 60 months, it just blew my mind. And once again I thought to myself I'd so much rather be me than them. Perhaps they are employed though, perhaps they aren't disabled, perhaps they have a significant other to help them out, or some other source. Still, I could afford what was determined for me and I was happy.

After we left the court, John I went to the Grill, which is a restaurant in Hemlock, and I ate half of my meal and saved the rest for dinner (my appetite still had not returned). After that we got back to my house and took my car to fill up the gas tank. It was only just slightly below half but I thought that since I had John there to help me out, I would take advantage of his help so long as he didn't mind.

John helped me bring my food and transfer chair in from the car, he told me to call him any time I needed anything, and then he left to run some more errands for his family. I went to my spare room, sat in my wheelchair, and put on a clean pair of sweats and a sweatshirt. I couldn't wait to get out of the clothes that I had worn to the hearing. I finally managed to make it to the couch where I sat down and waited for the tears to come. They never did, but I have to admit I felt like crying. I was so mentally drained and emotionally exhausted, I couldn't believe it. The worst part was over, or so I hoped. I didn't really want talk to anyone but I still talked to my dad about what was going on and explained the extent of the bankruptcy. The next day I woke up and I could have sworn I had a smile on my face, I didn't of course, but I sure could tell a weight had been lifted from my shoulders.

Several years ago a friend of mine's grandmother moved into an assisted-living facility. That year for Christmas I gave her a roll of quarters thinking that she could use them in the laundry facilities there. When she opened up the gift on Christmas morning she exclaimed, "Oh look, gambling money!" Clearly that was not what I had intended but as I sat there I thought to myself, "Well, they're her quarters now and she can do anything she wants with them."

At some point I had wished my parents would've helped me out by paying my medical bills because I knew they could have afforded it but it was their decision to make. They can do anything with their quarters that they want as well. After a couple of days I realized that my first payment to the court was going to come out on October 20, 2014, exactly one year after I went into the hospital only to come out 4.5 months later. I also decided that I shouldn't have been surprised that my parents didn't help me out with my medical bills. They had done a lot for me. They flew me to Florida to live with them while I recuperated, bought me a new computer while I was there, provided for me, and took me to my appointments. Some would say they didn't do anything for me that other families around the world wouldn't have done for their own family. That may be true, but if they had paid for my medical bills I would have been beholden to them for the rest of my life. Though I may not have a lot of money in the bank, it is my money. They are my quarters and I can do anything with them that I want. So in the end I guess bankruptcy really was the best thing for me. I mean after all, I can't file bankruptcy from my parents.

In early May I kept receiving documents from the bankruptcy court about the usual 'goings-on', but what I didn't expect was to find that my bankruptcy had been discharged. At first I was alarmed because when I looked it up on the internet, they said one reason for discharge could be because I had not been paying my monthly fee. That would mean I would owe the entire balance. I knew I had been paying from direct deposit out of my bank account. I could not figure out what I had done wrong. In the meantime, I had gotten yet another bill for over $1000 from a neurology office, issued before I went into the VA. I freaked out, checked my paperwork, and figured out that they had been named in my bankruptcy suit. I called my lawyer to find out what I should do. He told me I should take the bill to their offices and they would essentially send a 'cease and desist' letter. I don't know how much happier I could have been.

As for my case being discharged, it was, completely. Apparently no one named in my bankruptcy filed a claim against me. My lawyer's office told me to hold on to that piece of paper.

Thanksgiving

Thanksgiving 2014; I had returned my father's phone call to wish him a happy Thanksgiving. During this phone call I revealed to him that I wasn't planning on going anywhere that day since I had not gotten to bed until 6 AM that morning. I explained that my days and nights were mixed up if I didn't have to be someplace the next day. My sleeping pills didn't seem to be helping me. I told him that I had not gotten into the VA yet, although I had some phone calls that had not been returned. It was a nightmare trying to reach the VA via the phone. And lastly I told him that day for lunch I was going to have a Smart One and for dinner that night I would probably have some noodles. What I didn't tell my dad was that I had gone from Monday through Wednesday night that week without speaking to another human being – and I loved it!

Later that day, at about 0330 p.m., I got a voicemail from him asking me to call him back. It was important. By the tone of his voice I thought someone had died. Fortunately that wasn't the case. When I got him on the phone he thanked me for calling him back and then said he thought I should come back to Florida immediately. He cited my conversation earlier with them, stating that I wasn't sleeping well, I wasn't eating well, and I couldn't argue the fact that I wasn't getting the same amount of exercise. He went on to say that they never felt as if I should have left when I did and they wanted me to come back and stay indefinitely. I told him I couldn't afford it because I needed to replace my water heater. He said that if I went back to Florida I would not have to worry about my water heater. Then he said they would pay for the return flight. I asked him specifically for a round-trip ticket and he agreed. I asked him to give me until Tuesday the following week and then I would decide what I wanted to do– basically I told him I was going to try to get into the VA even if I had to go sit on the doorstep.

The next day I was at my friend Cheryl's house to 'help' her decorate her house for Christmas. That was kind of a joke since there wasn't much I could do, although I did help put the hangers on the ornaments. I am pretty sure it was a ploy to get me out of my house for a period of time, plus, I'm sure she could use the company. While I was there, my Dad left me a voicemail at 1110 a.m. stating that they had some flight schedules for me and I needed to call him back. This upset me because I had just talked to him the night before and asked him to give me until Tuesday, and he had agreed, now he was calling me the next morning. Less than two hours later I received another message from him – I was not picking up my phone at this point – and he left me a message that they had found a one-way flight, nonstop, out of Flint for $220. I was livid at this point. Cheryl said it sounded as if he wasn't treating me as an adult and that he should. She also said that I should have some say in when I go and how long I stay. I told Cheryl there had to be some sort of compromise, after all, I couldn't not go just to spite them but I didn't want to go and stay for another six months. Cheryl encouraged me to return his phone calls and I said "It could be ugly". She told me to call him just to tell him I received his messages and that I couldn't talk right then but I would call him back later to discuss my options. I did call him back and explained that I was at Cheryl's and I couldn't talk, but I'd call him back later. He asked me if I had received his messages to which I replied, "Yes, I did, which is why I am calling you now to tell you that I will call you back later." He replied that was okay with him, I could call back later, the next day, or after Tuesday. I didn't call him again until Tuesday after I figured out what my compromise was going to look like.

I think what upset me the most about the situation was that I had told them the truth about my life and they used it against me. From that point on I decided I wouldn't provide them that opportunity. Unless my activities landed me in a hospital, they didn't need to know.

Later that day, I decided to go to Rite Aid to get some cranberry-flavored Sprite. I thought it would go well with my turkey and mashed potato Smart One. When I got home I opened the door from the garage into the kitchen and I set my Sprite on the chair that I had placed there for groceries, so that I didn't have to pick them up off of the floor once I got into the house. I set the Sprite on its side and to my utter disbelief I watched it roll off of the chair, fall to the floor, and explode. The cap flew off the bottle and the soda pop came shooting out like a fountain. Some of the pop shot across through the air and hit my thigh. The rest of it pooled around on the floor. I could not believe my eyes. I stood there aghast. Since I'd been home everyone had told me to call them if I needed help. So as I stood there I thought to myself, "Who am I going to call to help me? Let me think, this is Thanksgiving evening, so that would be no one." So with 'no one' in mind I had to think of a way to do something. I sat on the chair for a few minutes contemplating my options. I knew I didn't want to track soda pop onto my living room carpet. My first objective was to get through the soda pop to the drawer in my kitchen that held some towels. That drawer happened to be on the other side of the kitchen, naturally. The other immediate issue I had was that I did not want to slip and fall in the soda pop. I had enough of a mess. Gingerly I made my way through the pond of soda pop, all the way to the far side of the kitchen, grabbed some towels, threw a couple on the puddle of pop and placed one strategically so I could get into the living room without tracking it into the carpet. Because I knew I couldn't stand up and drop towels on the floor, I went to the other room and got my wheelchair. Once in my wheelchair I went to the bathroom and grabbed several beach towels to toss on the floor to help soak up the soda. I figured it would do for one night.

I talked to Tracy that night to tell her about my dad's phone call. She agreed to go with me on Monday to the VA to get myself assigned a PA. I told her about the bottle of pop incident. When she realized that the incident had occurred indoors she chuckled and said she would come over on Monday and do a hot mop of the area, wash the towels, grab some lunch, do some shopping and of course visit the VA. Fortunately for me, a friend of mine, John, had called me the day before Thanksgiving to wish me Happy Thanksgiving. He asked me how I was getting along and told him I was doing okay and that I was learning to further work within my limitations. For instance, because my overhead garage door light was burnt out, I carried a flashlight in my car so that if I came home after dark I would be able to find my way around in the garage. He offered to come over on Saturday to change my lightbulb. Before he got there on Saturday I told him that I didn't have a ladder for him to use. So on Saturday he arrived with a ladder and I explained to him what had happened on Thanksgiving and that Tracy had agreed to come over and help clean the floor and wash the towels. By the end of his visit, he had changed on my lightbulb, taken the towels downstairs to be washed on Tuesday, and had done a once over on my floor where I had spilled so that I didn't walk on sticky stuff until Tuesday. He also took me to drop off my laundry and get my haircut while he ran errands of his own.

Tracy ended up coming over on Tuesday rather than Monday because she had a lengthy dental appointment Monday. She swept my entire kitchen floor and then poured some Pine-Sol into a bucket and hot mopped the entire floor, not just where I had spilled pop, even parts of the wall where the pop had splashed. She put the towels in the washing machine and then we left to run some errands. We stopped by my bank, we picked up my laundry, and we stopped at Wendy's to eat. Eventually we made it to the VA. I didn't know it at the time but the parking spot we got was a miracle compared to the future parking spots that my friends would find when they took me to the VA. We had taken my transfer chair because although I could walk with my cane I had a feeling it would be a long way to go. I didn't know where were going, so it was much simpler to take my own transfer chair. We got into the VA and I was surprised to see there were a set of stairs at the entrance. That struck me as odd because it seemed to me that during my 4 1/2 month stay, I saw so few people who were not in a wheelchair. Fortunately they had an elevator rather than a ramp. The man at the front information desk, had another person take us to the office of the man who would determine eligibility for medical benefits. It turned out that I was already enrolled but I had not been assigned a local physician's assistant, so he walked us to the woman who would assign me a team. She set me up for my blood work and my physical just two days from that day. I was surprised at how fast they could get me in – I didn't know how I was going to get there since I knew Tracy had to work – but I knew I had other options. Before we left that day, Tracy and I went to each station on various floors to make sure I would feel comfortable when I arrived on Thursday.

My neighbor Pat agreed to take me to the VA on Thursday. She dropped me off at the front door, helped me inside, and I was happy to find a transfer chair just waiting for me. It was a good thing she dropped me off because she had to park about as far away from the front door as she could get. I was able to get right in to get my blood work done and one of the men there was the phlebotomist who took my blood during my extended hospital stay. It was kind of nice to say hello and let him know how I'd been doing, where I'd been, and how I'd been feeling.

After my blood work was done, I realized that no one had told me I was going to have to provide a urine sample – which I found I could provide after my afternoon physical. Pat and I went to the cafeteria in the VA. While we were waiting in line I saw Sandy, my physical therapist during my stay. I waved to her and she came over to say hello before heading back to her office. While Pat and I were eating our lunch, another woman, Patty, recognized me and came over to our table. She had been one of the office assistants in the CLC where I stayed. She came over and told me she had heard I would be there that day. She hugged me, and told me I looked great. She was so happy to see me and asked if I was still living in Florida? I explained I had moved back and that I was getting back into this VA. She hugged me again and told me that she thought I looked really good and then went on her way. Pat and I sat in the cafeteria for quite a while because my next appointment was about an hour and a half away. As we left the cafeteria she needed to use the restroom. While I sat there waiting for her, one of the caregivers that I had during my stay spotted me and came over to say hello. She was amazed at how good I looked and told me to keep up the good work. She had to head back and I told her to tell everyone I said hello. After Pat was ready, we started to head to my next appointment. As I was starting out I was grabbed from behind and lo and behold it was Janine, another one of my caregivers. She had run from the CLC to the cafeteria because the other caregiver had told her I was there. We could only chat for a minute but she told me that she had received the note I had sent to everyone about how I was doing. I told her I would be in touch and we would talk later. I made it to my next appointment and I would have been on time had I been in the right line. I had been given some misinformation, but no worries, I figured out where I was supposed to check in electronically, and while I was in the middle of that, the nurse assistant found me and led me to the examination room. Pat sat in the waiting room.

During my exam I met with three people, the nurse assistant – who had to take a boatload of information about me, the physician assistant-in-training – she asked a lot of same questions and I told her that I would like to be considered for outpatient physical therapy, and I also needed to be scheduled for my next pelvic exam. It seemed as if I waited there for such a long time for my physician to show up. When she did, we discussed my medications, my physical therapy, my in-house inspection for safety, and she told me my blood work came back with extremely high sodium. She wanted me to be admitted to see if they could mitigate the high sodium. It turned out they let me go home and I had to drink a lot of water and return on Monday for additional blood work. After they gave me my discharge papers, I still had to do my urinalysis. Pat had waited for me for two hours, but she was a really good sport about it, especially because when we left they called transport services for us and she got a ride out to her van.

The following Monday John took me to the VA to have more blood work done. I asked the same phlebotomist why I had high sodium. He said, "Quit eating high sodium foods." I replied, "I guess I should get rid of that salt-lick next to my bed." The last time I gave blood for testing they had taken it from my right arm so I offered my left arm saying to him, "Take it out my left arm, I think there's less sodium over there." The following Monday the VA called and set up two appointments for me, one for physical therapy the next Tuesday and one for my pelvic exam January 30th. As it turned out I couldn't find a ride to the VA on that Tuesday so I rescheduled it for December 24th. It wasn't that I couldn't get there on my own but it wasn't until I rescheduled that I realized the entrance to the PT area was different than going in through the front door. I had secured a ride for 24th when Jane from the VA, who was an overseer of the OT area, called me and noted that I had canceled my appointment for that day. I explained to her why I had done that. She offered to sign me up for in-home care – PT/OT to which I readily agreed.

I asked her at that time about them coming in to do a safety check of my house and she said one of the OT would be doing that. I asked her if I didn't hear from them before the 24th should I go to my appointment? She said she didn't think it would take that long but yes, if I had not heard back, go to my appointment. Later that same day the VA contacted me again to let me know I had been recommended for in-home care and that an RN, dietitian, social worker, OT, and PT would be coming to my house. She said the OT and PT would come to my house for a minimum of 10 visits.

A few days after all of this, I got sick in my sink because I couldn't make it to the toilet. It took me almost 2 weeks to get some Drano. Also I dropped a cherry tomato on my kitchen floor. It landed next to the oven beneath the cupboard lip. I sat there and wondered how I was going to get at it. Finally I used my cane to coax it out to where I could grab it, but there was poor lighting and I couldn't feel my fingertips, so I couldn't just pluck it up. I used the "claw" method. I turned over my hand, opened my fist and viola there it was in the palm of my hand. I felt like I had performed a magic trick.

One of the best finds for a disabled person who can drive, is the discovery of a full-service gas station. My neighbor Cindy told me about one near us after I returned home from Florida. Prior to that, I was asking friends of mine to go with me to fill up my tank. I found out much later that some gas stations at the larger supermarkets have assist buttons that 'call' into the store from the pump and an attendant will come out to help you. I found another gas station in the area where, when you pull up and show your handicapped placard, they will come out and pump your gas for you. It seems like such a small thing, but it harkens back to the scope of one's world.

Martin Luther King's Day and Beyond

Compared to November, December went really well. A few people had invited me over to spend time with them during the holidays. I ended up with Cheryl and her family and it was a good time. I have been told that I depend on other people to make me feel comfortable in an unknown situation. Some people don't put it quite so kindly but I get the point. That night, though, I did pretty well.

As I was heading out to Cheryl's that afternoon for Christmas dinner, I remembered that recently, I had gone through a convenience store drive-through where one could purchase pop, chips, beer, wine and the like. While I was in line paying, the proprietor of the store noticed that I was running low on change in my little change bag. Due to my neuropathy, I normally hand over my bag of change and let them pick it out because I can't. As he was giving me my change back, he told me that he had filled my bag with quarters, dimes and nickels from his tip jar. I thought he meant he had changed my dollars into smaller change. But he hadn't, he had donated his money, his tips, for my little change bag. That realization brought me to tears.

During late December and early January, the home care providers from the VA had been making their rounds. Over the course of a week I met with my new home care nurse, social worker, dietitian, physical and occupational therapists. They had come out to assess the house for safety purposes, my mental status, my dietary needs and the course that my physical therapy would take. Within a few weeks after that, I had received a bench for my tub (the bench has a part that sticks out from the tub. As a result, when the shower curtain is closed, it looks like my tub is pregnant) a Versa frame (some armrests) for my toilet. At my OT's insistence, I had gone with my friend John to Walmart and picked up another nightlight for my bathroom and a slip-resistant mat for my tub. They also bought a stool for me to use in the kitchen because I couldn't stand up for as long as necessary to cook. When I sat down on a kitchen chair in front of the stove, it was too low for me to cook. They also had a new walker coming for me – one I could sit down on while tooling throughout the store. It also had brakes as well, which meant going down an incline would be more manageable. Given my continued lack of balance/coordination/endurance we pretty much determined that, for the time being, I was better off using a walker than a cane. Too bad I hadn't figured that out sooner.

Mid-January, with all this in the works, I was happy. I was starting new exercises. I had the goal of working up to being an outpatient physical therapy recipient at the VA, I was working on coordination, endurance, and balance. I couldn't believe what happened next.

It was late January 18th, which was a Sunday, and I had been watching football. I came out of my bathroom, using my cane as usual, when I lost my balance. Rather than pitch forward and hit my head on a table, or pitch backwards and hit my head on a copper pot, I sat down. Straight down. I'm pretty sure my left knee gave out underneath me since it had been giving me issues for years. I didn't give it much thought since as far as I knew, I had avoided major head trauma. I woke up at some point during the early morning hours and although I couldn't feel pain in my ankle – due to the neuropathy in my feet – I could see my left ankle had swollen a bit. It had begun to throb which was telling me something, since I couldn't feel anything below my knees on a regular basis. I couldn't decide what to do, it was close to 2 AM in the morning on the 19th. I thought I could go back to sleep and maybe get up at around 5 AM. The more I thought about it, I realized I probably shouldn't wait. I had told my friends and family that if I ever needed help, I would not wait. At about 3:15 AM I called 911, crawled to my front door, turned on the porch light and awaited the ambulance's arrival. After some careful inspection by the paramedics we decided it would be best if I went to the emergency room for further evaluation. They could tell how much it had swollen. I kept saying to them, "So you're saying I can't delay this?" One paramedic said to me, "If you were my daughter you'd be going in."

I was admitted to the emergency room at about 3:40 AM on January 19th, Martin Luther King Jr. Day. They took a series of x-rays of my foot and ankle, splinted my left foot and ankle, and advised me to follow up with a bone and joint specialist the next day. They prescribed me some medication for pain but I didn't have it filled because I didn't have insurance. The VA was closed that day due to the holiday and they wouldn't have filled a script from another source in any event (I found out later that I wasn't entirely correct about this – they did review my file and issued me their own script – which makes more sense in hindsight). Now, how was I going to get home? My ramp had not been installed yet, I didn't have my transfer chair with me. Not that that would've helped because it had little wheels that were harder to get over obstacles and I couldn't take a taxi. I called my friend John, he couldn't make it but he said his wife Holly would. Holly got me at about 7:30 AM. She had recently had surgery on her right wrist but somehow she was going to help me into the house. How, we had no idea. We went to the bone and joint clinic to see if I could get in but because I was with the VA, I couldn't get in without a VA referral. Holly enlisted the help of her daughter Jessica to get me back into my house. When we got there Holly got my transfer chair. Between the two of them they got me into my chair and wheeled me to the steps of my front door and then I hopped on one foot. With my arms around their shoulders, they basically carried me inside. They got me settled and because I was still on the pain meds from the hospital I wasn't in a whole lot of pain. I was exhausted from being up the night before, and the mental stress of it all, so I slept from about noon until about 0230 maybe. They had told me at the hospital not to put any weight on my left foot. Before Holly and Jessica left I made sure I could get into my bathroom using my transfer chair. If I couldn't get in there on my own, either they couldn't leave or I couldn't stay. It took a little effort and I marked up the hell out of my walls but I was able to do it on my own. As the afternoon wore on, and the medication wore off, my left foot hurt terribly. I didn't know it then but I had broken five bones in my foot and ankle. Later on, I was in so much pain that afternoon and evening I wanted to chew my own leg off. I didn't have any pain medication at all; no aspirin, no Motrin. Probably the worst thing about the entire first night was that, since the advent of my neuropathy, when I start to drift off to sleep I twitch. Because I was so exhausted that night I would drift off to sleep, and even though my foot was throbbing, I wasn't in pain unless I moved it. That first night when I would inadvertently twitch due to falling asleep, my left foot would jerk involuntarily. It felt like I had been hit with an electric shock. This went on the whole night every 20 minutes or so.

The next day, Tuesday, Tracy was coming over to make me some food that could be portioned out and frozen so I could just pop the food into the microwave. This way I didn't fill up on high-sodium frozen dinners from the store. The issue now was that I was unable to get the supplies, so I called her earlier that morning to let her know she was going to have to pick up the ingredients for cooking goulash and tuna casserole. She also dropped off my laundry and picked up some OTC pain medications for me later that day.

I also called my HBPC nurse, Karen, to relay my accident information. I didn't know if the accident-related bills would be covered i.e. the ambulance ride, the hospital care (x-rays, pain meds) and the pending bone doctor visit. And she couldn't tell me for certain. So I got online to see what requirements had to be met for the VA to cover non-VA bills. There were 10 requirements that needed to be met, three of the most pertinent to me were- notifying the VA within 72 hours of the incident (done), VA was not feasibly available at the time (it happened on a holiday); and a prudent layperson would have reasonably expected that delay in seeking immediate medical attention would have been hazardous to life or health (five broken bones). There was also quite a bit about health coverage in general, but essentially because I had been treated by the VA within the previous 24 months and I had no other health coverage, I should have been covered. Having said that, until I actually received word that my balance at MMR and St. Mary's was zeroed out, I was concerned.

Later that day, the HBPC OT stopped by to put together the bench for my tub in my bathroom.

Follow up- 21st Holly and Jess took me to the VA to get my pain meds on Wednesday. Of course the ramp to my front door had been ordered, but wasn't there yet. As a result Holly and Jess had to carry me in and out of the house. Once at the VA, I wasn't familiar with the process to get medication as an outpatient. For instance, I thought I could go right to the pharmacy window, but it doesn't work that way. I needed to scan my ID card at a kiosk first and wait to be seen by the pharmacist, then I had to wait until my name showed up on a T.V. screen letting me know my prescription was ready for pick-up. This process took a lot longer than anticipated, but in the end it all worked out. During the middle of this, Ray called me to tell me Pat was in the hospital for heart problems. I hadn't told them about my accident and it didn't seem like a good time then. He assured me Pat would be okay and I asked him to keep me posted.

My friend John took me to the bone doctor that Friday, the 23rd, and after some discussion with the doctor, a purple cast was applied. At that point the need for surgery was still unknown. Naturally John had to carry me in and out of the house- he used a fireman's carry- and he said, "I am glad you don't weigh very much." So over the ice and snow, and to his vehicle, he carried me. Once we returned to the house and he had me safely inside I said to him, "You know how people say 'I couldn't have done this without you.'? Well, I REALLY could not have done this without you!!!"

The following Monday, Jan 26ᵗʰ, a handicapped ramp to my front door was installed. Relief. That day was bitterly cold outside. They arrived around 8 AM and were done close to 10:30 AM. I was relieved because that meant in the event of an emergency, I would be able to get out of my front door without having to commando-crawl (or have people carry me). The ramp measured 20 feet in length. It was aluminum and had railings but I knew that when the temperature was warmer and the weather drier I would put some slip resistant tape down. I quickly learned that no one could sneak up to my house using that noisy ramp. Everyone who visits makes the same comment. I refer to it as my intruder alert.

On Jan 27ᵗʰ Tracy B. went grocery shopping for me. After I had fallen and broken my foot I had written to the girls I used to work with- Tracy B, Mary, Dianne, and Shelly to let them know what had happened. Tracy B had offered to do some grocery shopping for me and I knew it had to be quick because she was scheduled to travel to China in early February. This was the first time that someone outside my "usual circle" had shopped for me. Up until this point I had done really well maintaining my diet with things I already had in the house. From this point forward I would have to depend on people as they were available. For instance, when I needed ink for my printer so that I could print paperwork necessary for taxes due to my bankruptcy. I even had someone come over one time to help me unplug my toilet because I had no access to a plunger and even if I had at that point I couldn't have gotten to the toilet to plunge it. So I was learning that although there are things I needed to get done, sometimes what I needed simply did not fit into someone else's availability, capability, or willingness. And while we all know the world isn't all about us, there are times if you don't make it about you, things just don't get done. There is a happy medium and I know that. It's not just about finding the balance, sometimes it's letting other people know that you are trying to find a balance and that you are going to need their help.

On Wednesday, Jan 28th, my first caregiver, Sunshine, arrived. This was the first day since my accident that I had a caregiver come to the house to help me in and out of the shower. My caregiver had called in sick so they had sent someone else to come to my house on short notice. I wasn't quite sure what to expect but fortunately I was used to disrobing in front of complete strangers. I didn't know what to expect because I had been told that different caregivers would provide different services. Some of them would do light household chores, some would run errands, some would take me on errands, but essentially it was up to the caregivers themselves what they were willing to do outside of providing personal care. This woman's name was actually Sunshine. I remember telling her that her parents must have been really optimistic. She assisted me in and out of the shower. I had a kitchen garbage bag to put over my cast, sealing it at the knee to keep water off. Then she vacuumed my front room and her allotted time was up. My HBPC PT Lori stopped by at 4 p.m. to evaluate me, and while she was there, John dropped by to fix my toilet.

Friday, Jan 30th, Tracy took me to the Ann Arbor VA. This visit was for a follow-up appointment that I had scheduled because of benign fibroids discovered in Florida. My doctor and I agreed to schedule a checkup in six months to confirm that nothing had changed in that area. The appointment I was keeping in January was a result of that agreement. Tracy agreed to take me. The ride there gave Tracy and me some time together for which I was grateful. Tracy and I took a wrong turn on the way there and as a result we got there about five minutes late which in military time means only 25 minutes early. However, the day was nice, the weather was clear, and everything went off without a hitch. I would hear the results later. When we got closer to home we stopped at a local produce market and I stocked up on fruits and vegetables. It was nice to be the out of the house since, other than going to a doctor's appointment on occasion, I hadn't been out of the house since January 23.

Feb 2nd my new care giver, Pansy, arrived late due to a snow storm. She was on time but stuck in the street since the plows hadn't been through yet. She helped me in and out of the shower, cleaned my bathroom, and vacuumed again. Pansy is originally from Jamaica and her accent is so thick – even after seven years in the States- that understanding her is difficult. If she speaks slowly enough I can catch about half of what she says clearly, but if she's 'on her soap box', I can only catch about a third. No worries, we make it work.

Feb 3rd My HBPC nurse, Karen stopped by. She asked if I was in any pain, checked out my blood pressure, my pulse and just generally inquired about how I was getting along. My friend Kay came by for lunch later, and my friend Nyla brought me dinner that night.

Feb 4th My neighbor Cindy took me to my bone doctor and the x-ray revealed a ct scan was necessary and surgery was still a possibility.

Feb 5th OT stopped by, and the grab bars for my bathroom were installed by an independent contractor.

Friday Feb 6th Pansy brought some rubber bands, used in the supermarket on broccoli, to help seal the plastic bag around my cast while I showered and then she did some of my laundry in my basement.

Wed Feb 11th I played 'tag' between the bone doctor's office and the VA. The bone doctor said they faxed the paperwork to the VA necessary for me to have a CT scan locally, my VA contact didn't receive it because it went to the wrong office at the VA, so I called the bone doctor back with a different fax number. The VA finally called me to let me know they got the correct paperwork to get records to submit a referral.

Thurs. Feb 12th My dad phoned me from Florida to tell me he received a phone message from the Detroit VA to schedule me an MRI (not a CT scan and not local).

Fri Feb. 13th I called Detroit and scheduled an appointment on Feb 18th. Laurel agreed to drive me.

Wed Feb 18th For the trip to Detroit, we took my car since hers was in need of repair. We got a late start and there was a lot of traffic and several accidents due to the inclement weather. I called ahead to tell them I was running late. All went well once we got there and we had a safe ride home. Before she left for the day Laurel made chili and mac 'n cheese dishes for me and put them in the freezer. We talked a lot about her addiction issues that day – she had been struggling with food addiction for years and had recently sought treatment. What she was experiencing was similar to what I had gone through with my addiction, with one major difference, she had to eat. I was struck by the enormity of what she was going through… the extent of her discomfort, the anguish and helplessness she had felt. I had no idea. I told her I was proud of her because she cared enough to change. She thanked me and she confided in me more. I thought about it a lot the next day and while I know I lacked the tools to help her, I was singularly happy and relieved to know she found support/comfort with the help of, and in the company of, others. Which really drove home the fact that she didn't really need me (as I put it; her 25 new best friends leap-frogged me). One upshot to that sobering, yet depressing, thought was the realization that I couldn't let her down.

I know it's not about me, and I've always told her that I can't ask for the truth and then beat her up for it, but after some thought, I have to believe that she had to have known that after she confided in me, the light bulb would pop on in my head. She told me a little about her eating habits prior to her beginning this program she's on. I wondered who knew before her journey began 5 months prior to our conversation? I understand her fear, shame, embarrassment, and I understand why she didn't feel like she could confide in me. I get that, and in all honesty, I couldn't have provided the support she needed. I don't begrudge her any of that.

What stuck with me though is the memory of our prior conversations when she advised me to take my addiction into the light (reveal it to others) because then it would (allegedly) have no hold over me. She was a hypocrite at best at that point. But even that isn't what really rubbed me raw. What really got to me was that she aired my business to her family, all of them, and 'her' church which I had attended for a time. I overlooked that because I knew she needed someone to talk to…but to talk about me, as if she had no issues of her own, that seriously needed to be dealt with, just slayed me.

As recently as our trip to Detroit (2/18/15) I actually thought to myself that I was glad I had gotten to know her before I took sick in 2013. That was a year and a half into our friendship. Here it was a year and a half later and I realized I didn't really know her at all. Laurel and I have since discussed all of this and we are on good terms. I have been asked by other friends about my situation with her, and while I admit sometimes I don't understand her (or her me) and I scratch my head in wonder, I can honestly say this- she has never been malicious toward me. Friends are not perfect – to expect such a thing is to invite disappointment.

Feb 23rd I was called to set up a phone consultation with my PA from the Saginaw VA for February 25th. I was led to believe it was for the MRI of my left foot. There had been some confusion after my visit to the bone doctor on February 4th because my orthopedic doctor had recommended a CT scan from St. Mary's Hospital. Instead, my father had received a phone call from the Detroit VA to schedule me an MRI. In any event, I was eagerly waiting to hear what happened with my foot. My doctor was an hour late calling me which was no big deal, where was I going to go? My PA started the phone call by talking to me about my abdominal test results from January. Apparently they had found a mass in my left fallopian tube that needed further evaluation. I was stunned. We talked about medications that I would have to be given prior to my next MRI in Detroit and upping my sleeping medication because I had start upping the medication on my own when I couldn't sleep through the night. At the very end she asked me if I had any other questions and I asked her about my foot. She said to me, "What about your foot?" So after some review she told me that I would have to get a disk of the MRI and take it to my orthopedic doctor for him to review. I got the gist of information, but due to the news she had relayed to me about my left fallopian tube, I was in tears before I got off the phone. I texted Tracy with the information. She texted me back, asking me if I was okay, and I told her I wasn't, but I would take some medication that would calm me down. She called me later to make sure I was okay and again later that evening for the same reason. They weren't long conversations by any stretch of the imagination, but she had said to me, "We will get through this Pam, trust God, have faith." She also made the point that I was better off finding out exactly was going on so I knew what I was dealing with.

The VA called me back later to tell me that I could pick up my own MRI results from medical records prior to my appointment with the bone doctor. I called the bone doctor's office to schedule an appointment. When I called back the next day to let them know that they could request my MRI results from the VA, they informed me that my next appointment was void because I didn't have a referral from the VA. Also, they wouldn't request my MRI results because they should have been included with the referral.

So I was reeling from the news about my abdomen, dealing with authorizing and scheduling an appointment with the bone doctor, and that day I received the forms in the mail to fill out for my disability reassessment.

Here's the thing about each issue, yes they wanted to schedule me an MRI in Detroit. The last time they had tried to schedule me an appointment in Detroit, they didn't have my phone number and they called my father in Florida. The first thing I had to do was call my dad and let him know he might be receiving a phone call. Add to that, I did not know how I was going to get to Detroit since I couldn't drive myself with a cast on my foot. I had no idea who to call to get authorization to have my foot looked at by the doctor who had treated me in the first place. I couldn't fill out the disability reassessment forms because my handwriting was illegible. I asked Laurel if she could come over and help me fill out the forms. She told me her kids were in town from school that week and that she would be unavailable to help me to any appointments. She could not help me with my paperwork until March 9th.... but the paperwork was due March 11th. She thought it was fine if I sent it off one day before was due but I didn't. I called someone else who agreed to help me an entire week earlier. Laurel had asked someone else from 'her' church to take me to my appointments, and while I appreciated the thought, the person she volunteered lived an additional 30 minutes farther away than she did. I didn't find it feasible to ask someone to drive an hour to take me to a 15 minute appointment, or worse, a 2 hour drive to Detroit.

Cast off and wait

My cast came off in March. They put a "walking boot" on in its place and I erroneously believed walking would be easier. I had been told by one of my HBPC caregivers that walking with the boot would take some getting used to; that turned out to be the understatement of the year. When the bone Dr. authorized this new boot, he asked me if I had any questions. I said to him, "All I really want to know is if I am allowed to climb down the two steps into my garage so that I can get into my car?" He said that was fine, I thought I was golden, I was wrong. Walking in a boot for the average person must be tedious but for me, with my neuropathy, it was treacherous.

After I got home from the doctor that day I called my dad to tell him I was cast-free, I texted a friend or two the same information and then I grabbed my purse and my cane, locked the wheels of my wheelchair, and opened the main door to my garage. Like always, I backed down my steps gingerly and then I was faced with a problem, I had to figure out a way to pivot on my boot so that I could turn around and head towards the car but my balance was so off, even with the cane, that I needed two hands to steady myself. Luckily for me an empty box was strategically placed on end and it was just the right height for me to use as a point of balance. Then I caned my way over to the car and used that for balance with my cane in the other hand. I was so happy to wiggle myself into the car and be out on the road. The first thing I did was go to the full-service gas station and get my gas tank filled. I drove to get some sort of pop, realizing too late that I had an additional challenge when I got home. How in the hell was I going to carry anything in the house if I needed both hands to steady myself and not tip over? The answer came to me in a flash; whatever I took home was going to have to fit in my purse. Eventually, I found a black bag, akin to a mailbag, that I slung over my shoulder. For major hauls I still need help getting to the grocery store, into the grocery store, and through the line. Then whoever is with me has the additional chore of getting my groceries into my house. I put them away for myself, though.

In the midst of all this excitement, I was waiting to have the MRI of my fallopian tubes. I was all set to go, but a week after my cast came off, I sat down in my wheelchair and somehow twisted my bad ankle. The morning I was supposed to go to the VA for my transport to the Detroit VA, I was in too much pain. I suppose I could have wiggled myself into my car but I wasn't confident that I could make it from the VA parking lot, to where I needed to go inside the building, without further injury. As a result I called and rescheduled my appointment. I wasn't happy about it but the more I thought about it, I knew I had made the right decision.

In April, on the morning I was to go for my MRI the second time, I had my neighbor drop me off and then pick me up when I got back. My rationale was since I had to be there so early in the morning it would still be dark. That meant that I wouldn't be able to see my feet and walking would be a problem. In the end we took my transfer chair which turned out to be a good thing because at the Detroit VA they don't have volunteers to get you where you need to be. It would have been one hell of a hike. The MRI went well enough. I had taken my medication to calm me down for the procedure and it's a good thing too, because I was in there longer than they said I would be. If it was necessary, then it had to be done. About a week before my MRI the VA called me to schedule an appointment with my provider. I called back to schedule my appointment and asked them what it was for? And they said they didn't know. I asked them if I needed to have blood work done. And they said "no". I had scheduled my appointment for 0930 in the morning. I figured I could get there early enough to get a good parking spot and by 0930 it would be light out so I could see my feet. Then the day before my appointment, they called to tell me I needed lab work done. That meant I had to be there two hours earlier. I was pissed. I called my neighbor again and she agreed to drop me off and then pick me up afterwards. I wasn't upset that I had to get blood work done; I was upset because they waited till the last-minute to tell me. I figured it was one thing if they wanted to mess with my schedule, but because I could not plan ahead, I had to ask someone at the last-minute to take me and interrupt their plans.

The doctor's appointment went well overall. After my blood work, I went to the cafeteria and grabbed a bottle of water and a great big chocolate muffin. I spotted my social worker from the months I was in the VA and we talked for a bit and caught up on what had been going on. One of the caregivers that I had while I was in, stopped by to say hello to me and then as she left, Mary from OT came in to visit with me. Staci, the social worker, had told her I was in the cafeteria until my appointment at 0930. It was good to see Mary again and I told her I had planned to stop by after my appointment. She encouraged me to do that, telling me that everyone wanted to see me.

The visit with my doctor revealed a few things. I had extremely low cholesterol, low potassium, and my MRI results came back good. After some discussion I was sent back to have more blood work done to check my vitamin D levels and after she reviewed my medication, she asked me if I had accessed the VA's mental health. I asked her, "Could you be more specific?"

Two of the medications that I'm on concerned her because one is for anxiety and the other is for PTSD. She asked me if she could have Gwen, the social worker from mental health, send me some information. I told her that would be fine. Later that afternoon, I received a phone call from her, my PCP, and I had to call back the next day to get the test results, which made no sense to me. But I called back the next day anyway and I found out that I was going to be scheduled for an endometrial biopsy, more follow up blood work to check my potassium and vitamin D levels. I was also to continue on with the physiatry examination. The second round of blood work from that day revealed that the vitamin D levels in my blood were extremely low (>4) so she prescribed me a once a week supplement of 50,000 units for 3 months.

The next day Gwen called me and said that she thought I should come in and see her. I told her that my understanding was that she was going to send me some information. She said, "That's not normally how it works." And I told her about having a boot on my foot and not wanting to get there in the dark when I can't see my feet. I gave her a summary of my history with the VA. She said she would review my file and get back with me the next week.

I had been in contact with Gwen again and we arranged to meet on a Thursday at 1:30 PM. I had some things going for me, first of all I knew where I was going, not knowing can sometimes be a challenge. I had beautiful weather, and I had plenty of time to get to my appointment. I was worried about having to park in the back 40, so I got there incredibly early. I knew my endurance wasn't what it had been before I broke my foot, so after I parked in a great spot, and oddly, not even a handicapped spot, I made it to the front door of the facility and sat on the bench for the remainder of my wait. I was checked in and in the waiting room by five minutes after 1 PM. At 1:45 PM I called Gwen in her office and asked if I had gotten the time or date incorrect. She apologized, explaining that the appointment had not been put on her calendar. Once I was settled in her office I filled out some questionnaires and we determined that my anxiety level had been giving me the most difficulty. We talked for about an hour and she asked me what kind of therapist I wanted, what exactly was I looking for in a therapist? She mentioned the two men who had come to visit me while I was in the hospital on behalf of the VA mental health department. She asked me why I hadn't cared for them. I thought about my time with Anne, the therapist I had seen during my employment, and shortly thereafter. What was the difference? And it dawned on me, I wanted to feel like I mattered, Anne had done that for me, and those two men had not. In fact my comment was, "I don't really care if I matter to them, I just want to feel like I do." It's like that old saying, "You don't have to take someone's advice to make them feel good, just ask for it." We talked about my relationships within my family, about my birth mother who had passed away about 10 years before. I had long ago come to the conclusion that regardless of how much time we had left, we never would've gotten any closer. I asked my dad one time how long she had been dead and his reply was, "Not long enough."

We talked about my parents and I indicated that I thought we had a pretty strong relationship. I certainly wouldn't change it

I left that day glad that I had gone in. On the way out, I sat down on the bench outside the VA and took in the glorious sunshine.

I was able to take the walking boot off permanently after my bone doctor's appointment on April 27. I drove myself to the appointment thinking I could use my walker because the doors were automatic and I wouldn't have to wrestle with them to get in or out. It turned out I was overly ambitious. When I got to the building I realized that not only was the walking boot foot unwieldy (I had been maneuvering a wheelchair up to that point), I was really out of shape. It was exhausting. I had mostly sat in a chair for the past four months. Now I had to walk into an office, then to the x-ray machine, back to the examination room and out to my car. It was shockingly difficult. Once I was in the examination, room the doctor asked me how wearing the boot was going and I said, "Are you kidding me? It's a nightmare." He asked me if it was because of the boot itself or if it was because I was in pain? I told him it had nothing to do with pain and everything to do with the cumbersome boot. He told me I didn't need to wear it anymore, and as far as exercise went, I could do anything except jog. I chuckled to myself thinking how very unlikely that would be. I let him know that I had a regular shoe in the car and he asked me if I was going to put on as soon as I got into the parking lot. I replied, "Yeah, and then I thought I'd jog home." He said that he didn't see any need for a follow-up visit and wished me well. During checkout I asked the lady behind the desk if someone could help me with the door to the waiting room. As she opened the door she also wished me well and I bit back my response which would've been, "No offense, but I hope never to see you people again." I am sure that lots of people have that sentiment, but regardless of how I phrased it, it would have been offensive and that just didn't seem right.

It took me a few minutes once I was in the car but I got that boot off and my sock and shoe on before I left the parking lot. Arriving home with my foot free, I didn't know quite what to expect when I got out of my car. The first thing I did was throw the boot on my garage floor and then I gingerly stepped out, using my cane and the car for support. When I stepped out of the car one thing became obvious – the muscles in my ankle and foot had atrophied immensely. Putting my left foot down I had to really concentrate to make sure I didn't turn my ankle. I couldn't just stand there. It took some time but I made it into the house and back to my wheelchair. I knew I had a long way to go before my foot would ever be back to the way it was before my accident in January. The upside was I was already in physical therapy so wasn't something that had to wait and I could get to it right away. The other benefit to having the boot off my foot was that I no longer had to lie on my back to sleep!

I had an old fridge in my garage removed to give me more room to get around. It had always been difficult to get groceries from my car to the house. With this fridge removed, my home-based occupational therapist and I were able to set up a process using my walker that has brakes and a seat. I can step down using my cane and the grab bars next to the door, pivot towards my walker, and use that to get to my car. With my car door open to offer me support, I then fold one side of the walker out of the way and get into my car. Using this method, I am very easily able to transfer groceries and the like from my car to my house. It's a relief.

May 1st was the day my endometrial biopsy was scheduled at the Ann Arbor VA. I had debated driving myself to the Saginaw VA to catch the bus that morning and then using my walker to get to the transfer spot. I knew I needed the practice and the exercise. My concern was that once I got to the Ann Arbor VA I had no idea how far I was going to need to walk to get to my appointment. My appointment was scheduled for 0230 that afternoon but I had to leave at 0730 to catch the ride. I talked it over with both of my home care therapists and we decided that I would be better off not to take any chances. I decided to have Pat drop me off in the a.m. and I would use my transfer chair. It turns out that was the correct decision because when I got to the VA the office I needed to get to it would have been nearly impossible with my foot in such bad condition. It was so far away that I told the volunteer who escorted me to the office that it would have taken me until 0230 just to get to my destination. The path we took was so confusing that it dawned on me that I should have had some bread crumbs to drop on the floor leaving a trail so I could find my way back.

As I was checking in at 0930 in the morning I mentioned to the clerk that if they had an opening before my scheduled appointment I would be in the waiting room. She told me I could take her 12 o'clock spot because she had forgotten about it and wasn't prepared for it. I thanked her profusely. I was really happy about this for two reasons. One, I was the last appointment for the day which means the other four riders were waiting for me to leave. Two, the procedure was one of those things that you dread having to get done but once you're there you just want it to be over with. It reminds me of going to the dentist.

As I waited I started reading a new book. I was happy to have this because, every now and then, I find that when you are a captive audience in the waiting room, you invariably get stuck with someone who irritates you. I try not to be that person – but we are all someone else's idiot. I was happy to have this book along so that this idiot wouldn't be compelled to talk to me. Everyone who sat down next to him heard about all of his ailments, all of his wife's ailments, and the fact he suggested the doctors prescribe him cyanide. Listening to him really drove home the fact that I'd rather be me.

They came and got me at about 1230. Getting undressed without help was tricky enough but I managed. I only took my sweatpants off of my right leg so that I didn't have to deal with my left leg and foot. I explained to my doctor and nurse that I had only just recently regained the use of my left foot. The truly difficult part was trying to keep my left foot in the stirrup because it tended to want to shake side to side as my muscles were too weak to hold it in one spot. The procedure went as planned and I was out of there a little after 1 PM. As I headed to the front to check out, I asked them to call for an escort to take me back up front. The driver of the transport bus happened to be standing there. He had come by to check on me and offered to take me up front. As we were heading out he asked me if I remembered him from the night I broke my foot. He had been one of the responders that morning. I said to him, "So you would have been really surprised if I had walked in here with a walker." And he commented, "Yeah, you were in pretty rough shape."

On May 6 I received the news that my biopsy had come back clear. No cancer, no pre-cancer, just plain old menopause. I was so happy and relieved. I called my parents first, and then a few other friends, and sent an email out to some others. I have to admit I was feeling pretty empowered, being able to maneuver on my own, microwaving on my own, bathing and toileting on my own. I had been home long enough to know what my options were when I needed help, like putting a new screen door on or taking my vacuum cleaner in for repair. I was proving to myself that I was adaptable. Then that night, a fuse tripped in my basement and knocked the power out in my living room. I couldn't believe it. It occurred to me that even if I was dumb enough to try to maneuver the stairs I had no way to get to the far corner of my basement. I had to call for help realizing quickly I wasn't nearly as independent as I wanted to be or thought I was. I called my friend John because I hadn't seen him in a while, not since he had installed the ink in my printer, and because I like to spread the pain around and not depend on just one person. While John was over fixing my fuse box, and I can't tell you how relieved I was it was just a blown fuse, I told him that I considered trying to do it myself but I thought better of it. His comment to me was, "And can you imagine what we would have said to you had you tried?" And when I was talking to Tracy about it later she said to me, "What I want to know is if you would have taken your cell phone with you?"

My friend Kay had filled out the third-party redetermination paperwork for my disability the first week of May. Waiting around was tense. Everyone I talked to told me they would be really surprised if they didn't determine in my favor. I appreciated their support but I kept thinking to myself – your surprise is not going to help me pay my bills. I kept my mouth shut. I have often said to people, "If you think what comes out of my mouth is bad, you should hear what goes on in my head." Then on June 1st, I received notification that they had found my disability to be continuing. They didn't indicate when they would review my case again, only that they would review it from time to time. I was so relieved I was almost in tears. I called my dad first and then I called Kay. As I said to more than one person, it was odd for me to wish to be found disabled, given my work history. On the other hand, I'd rather be found disabled and receiving benefits, then be disabled and not receiving benefits.

After this I moved forward with other plans that I had been putting off until I knew I had money coming into the bank. Things like getting my carpets cleaned, getting a new water heater, and getting my garage floor fixed. My dad had been after me to get that floor fixed for years, especially given the condition I am now in with reduced feeling in my feet. Some water had gotten underneath my garage floor and caused it to heave, resulting in about a four-inch lip at the entrance. My dad was afraid, and rightly so, that I would gun the engine to get over the lip and not be able to brake before hitting the kitchen wall. I told my dad I felt he had a valid argument but I wasn't going to empty out my bank account when I didn't know if anything else was going in there. Grudgingly he said he understood.

A new beginning-

Or thank God...I'm disabled.

Once my disability redetermination came back in June and they found my disability to be continuing, I felt relieved, naturally, but I also felt as if I had been put through the wringer. No doubt, there was a lot of work to be done on my part to continue to improve physically. A few days after I got that good information, my physical therapist stopped by to lead me through some exercises. It was a beautiful day outside, so one of the first things she did was get my walker from my car. She wheeled me down the ramp from my house in my wheelchair and when we got to the bottom near my driveway she hooked the gait belt around my waist and I walked several paces, sat down for a bit on my wheelchair, and after a few more trips up and down my driveway, I walked back up my ramp and into my house. I said to her, "I feel like a puppy." Pat and Ray were sitting outside their garage and commented that they could see improvement.

I felt it was time to move on and get my carpets cleaned. I got the name of a local guy from my HB OT. It occurred to me as I was driving down the road, on my way to a drive-through "stop-and-rob", that although I like to be on my own and solely independent, having the networking capability and resources that the VA has provided me, either by design or God's will, has really come in handy. Who could ask for more?

Something else occurred to me as I was parking in a handicapped spot that day. I saw a person who looked fairly able-bodied leave the store, jump in his car, and drive away. Since I've had this condition, people who are not handicapped and park in a handicapped spot really piss me off. What upsets me even more are the people who are no longer handicapped and still taking advantage of the situation. One might argue a non-handicapped parking abuser doesn't know what they're doing, what they're taking away from those who need it. All formerly handicapped persons know exactly what they're doing and that is reprehensible.

I was able to get my carpets cleaned in mid-June and I decided at that point to put my wheelchair in my spare bedroom and begin using my walker from that point on around the house. I now had a basket for it so I could carry items much easier. When I first started using the walker again, it occurred to me pretty quickly that I had to think ahead whenever I would go to the kitchen to get food or supplies because I didn't want to have to make two trips. I was amazed at how fatigued I was, doing just that little bit of walking. It would get better and I realized that I had to go back to the 'pre-broken foot' house set up. This meant I had my wheelchair in my changing room so that I could access everything in my dresser drawers without risking tipping over. This also meant that I had to strategically place chairs in my kitchen again, one next to the main door to my garage and one in front of my refrigerator. The nice thing about the basket on my walker was that it has an insert for a cup or a bottle of liquid and I don't have to worry about it spilling. That is essential since I just had my carpets cleaned.

It was shortly after I started walking around the house again that I realized the seal on my toilet was leaking. I figured this out because when my caregiver was cleaning my toilet and flushed it, I could hear water hitting the concrete in my basement. I freaked out but not for long. I looked online for the cost of a plumber and discovered it would cost anywhere from $200 to $500. Then I got to thinking who to call for help? I knew one thing for sure, I wasn't going to be the person changing the seal. I called Tom and he quickly found a guy where he worked who would help change the seal for $50. They did a great job!

So I was out of the wheelchair. I typically only used my travel chair at this point when I knew that the distance to my destination would be more than I would be able to walk comfortably.

My home-based primary care was starting to discharge me. I had made it to the goal of outpatient physical therapy at the VA. I could still maintain a caregiver to help me with personal care and light housekeeping duties indefinitely, but I felt that might be coming to an end as well. In mid-June, I saw my in-home physical therapist for the last time as well as my social worker who stopped by to see how I was getting along. She wanted to let me know if I ever needed anything to give one of them a call and she also gave me the number of the VA person who is the liaison to Compassionate Care, the company that provides caregivers, in case I ever wanted to reactivate their services.

Also in late June, I was discharged by my in-home OT and nurse. I had actually graduated to a roll-about chair in my kitchen which would replace the stationary chair from my refrigerator and allow me to sit at a proper height to cook my own food. At this point, I'm pretty sure I will never attempt baking. It has a lot to do with the lack of feeling in my hands but also it was never my thing before I became ill.

One of the recommendations from my VA PA visit in May was that I be scheduled for a Physiatry exam at the VA in Ann Arbor. They scheduled it for me in late May. When I called to request transportation from the Saginaw VA to my appointment in Ann Arbor, my call was answered by a recording saying that unless it was an emergency they wouldn't be providing transportation to Ann Arbor or Grayling. So I called and left a message in Ann Arbor that I wouldn't be able to make my appointment. They returned my call and we rescheduled my appointment for the third week of June. That turned out to be an interesting day.

Because I knew exactly how far I was going to have to go once I got on site, I decided I'd be better off taking my travel chair. My appointment was set for 8:30 AM which meant I would have to be at the Saginaw VA at 5:30 AM. My neighbor Pat was kind enough to drop me off at about 20 minutes after 5 AM. There were a couple of veterans also waiting and they were decidedly disgruntled. On one hand, I didn't want to listen but on the other hand it was really interesting. The first man wore a red shirt and had apparently spent the night on the bench in front of the VA. He had quite the history but the other guy was convinced his own PTSD was caused because he spotted Bigfoot while he was in the military. His wife even divorced him because she feared him while he slept. Redshirt wasn't going with us to Ann Arbor, he was going to stay and talk to the director of the VA, or so he thought – I wonder how well that worked out for him. The other man got on the bus with the rest of us and I never heard another word from him. The nurse that travelled with us that day recognized me from my stay 21 months before.

Once we got to our destination they wheeled me to the front desk. I was a little confused about where I was supposed to go because the card they sent me in the mail indicated my appointment was in section 17 – but if it was on a Thursday or Friday then I was to go to section 14. At the front desk, I told him my appointment was for physiatry. This earned me a few quizzical looks. When the guy at the desk was looking it up in the book he asked me, "Does that start with an F?" It was legitimate question. I still wasn't sure what it meant because when they looked up my name in the computer, they said there were no appointments scheduled for me that day. I told him I had verified the fact I was going to be there through an automatic phone service two days before. So they wheeled me down there to find out what was going on. By the time we got to section 117, it was 8 o'clock on the nose. That's when we discovered the clinic had been canceled for the day 10 minutes prior. I couldn't believe it. The volunteer who had escorted me had the presence of mind to ask if I could get any proof that I had been there. I guess some people use the shuttle to get to town and shop, never having an appointment at the VA at all. I wasn't really upset when I consider the high rate of no-shows when it comes to people not showing up to their own appointments. I read that the no-show rate is between 5 and 55% which is why the doctors charge you a no-show fee if you haven't canceled before 24 hours. I figured it could have been worse. At least I had not come from Grayling. My escort and I saw my driver and told him what had happened. He let me know that an earlier bus would be heading back and I could be on it. He just didn't know when the bus would be heading out. So I bought myself a bottle of water and found a little table next to the coffee area. I was in for a long wait but boy, was it interesting watching people and hearing snippets of conversation. I had not been there very long when an older man asked if he could sit with me while he had a cup of coffee and waited for his appointment to have his blood drawn. He was a nice guy, his name was Dave, and we talked about books, TV shows, renters and some about travel. He only lived 4 miles from the hospital. This came up when I told him why I was there that morning. After he left, a woman came up with a book cart. Apparently anything on the cart was considered free and they only accepted books that were in good condition. They'd had an issue with people donating moldy books. It reminded me of food collection drives were people empty out their pantry, donating the worst of the worst. So at one point this young guy walked up to the book cart, saw a deck of cards, put them in his pocket and selected a few books. I don't think he was there for more than two minutes. Not five minutes later, the book woman said to some regulars, "Well, I was going to play solitaire, but I can't find my cards." She left the book cart and came back 10 minutes later with a new set of cards, sat at 'my' table, and began playing solitaire. Dave came back and kept offering her unsolicited advice. It didn't seem to bother her and then about 11:00 AM, she wished me a good day and took the book cart away. I felt bad for her because she had her sweater on inside out. I kept thinking, if it were me, would I want someone to tell me or would I rather believe no one had noticed?

At about 11:30 AM, the nurse from the bus was escorting her charge through the lobby and stopped to ask me if I wanted to join them for lunch in the cafeteria. I said I would and she found a volunteer to escort me to the cafeteria and through the pay line. The thing about hanging out with the caregivers is they all know each other. They've worked together for years which results in a huge feeling of camaraderie; much like being in the military or law enforcement. So sitting with the group of them at lunch is a lot like being behind the scenes at Disneyland. You get to see how things really get done, or, maybe the most effective way things get done. There were six of us at the table that day, three caregivers and three patients and was it hilarious! At one point Patty asked me if I was from Saginaw and I told her I was and she said, "You're the one whose appointment was canceled 10 minutes before you got there." Apparently my predicament had spread like wildfire.

When I found my appointment had been canceled I thought to myself that God must've had a reason for me being there that day. As we were preparing to leave LeeAnn, one of the other caregivers at the table, came around to get her charge and asked me, "Pam didn't you go to live with your parents?" I said, "Yes I did." We talked about that for little bit and she also remembered me from my brief 4.5 months at the VA. She said to me, "You are a miracle. You know, I didn't think you were going live." I replied, "Really?" And she said, "Yeah, I went home and prayed for you every night." Then she leaned over and gave me a good firm hug.

I was stunned, but I wasn't sure what surprised me more, that she remembered me after all that time or that she thought I was a dead person waiting to happen.

As the days went by, and one by one my primary home care people said goodbye I was relieved but somewhat unused to being alone again. It took me so long to get used to them being in my home on a regular basis so maybe I was a tiny bit sad. But that didn't last long – I was now able to eat Cheetos in my underwear if I wanted to. The next question was what to do about Pansy? After her trip to Jamaica, we went to her coming over once a week.

My VA outpatient OT and PT assessments were scheduled for July 14th. I had done my homework and knew exactly where I needed to park, keeping in mind that because it was at 1 PM in the afternoon I might have a long way to walk. By now I was pretty familiar with how things worked with the parking shuttle and I knew there was a number I could call to have them send the shuttle to me in the parking lot. At this point, all I really knew was that I would have to call the main number, ask for the Transportation Department, and hope for the best. I was lucky though and I was able to park within walking distance for me. As I was approaching the entrance doors to the CLC, one of the nurses I had known for my time at the VA hospital was also walking in and came over to give me a hug. I told her I would have hugged her back but I would've had to let go of my walker and I didn't want to tip over. As she and I were talking, an attendant pulled up beside me on a scooter and asked me if I would like to use that for my visit. I told him I didn't know what I would do with my walker and I didn't know how to operate a scooter. He told me he could put my walker behind the desk area of the lobby and then he showed me how to operate the scooter. Because there was more than one place I wanted to visit that day, I took him up on his offer. What a blast! As I was passing him by on my way to my assessments I told him I wanted some streamers for my scooter – the kind we put on bikes when I was a kid. He told me they had done that for Flag Day. And I said, "Well, I guess I missed out." I managed to get to the elevator without incident and they wanted to hold the door for me but there was someone already in there on a scooter. I told him to let him go. The guy said there was plenty of room and motioned for me to join them. I said to them, "Well okay, but I am a first time driver and I have no idea what I'm doing." The tricky part, aside from maneuvering doorways, was backing up. I made it to my appointment 35 minutes early and I was only the second one in the room. Over the next 35 minutes the room filled with about 10 other people. All of us had an appointment at 1 o'clock. While we were waiting, a man with his father, who was also on a scooter, said to me from across the room, "Ma'am, I think my dad could beat you in a race with your scooters." To which I replied, "You might be right, but I'm a first time driver, so I'm still pretty reckless."

The assessments went really well and in each one I had to state my goals. That's the thing about physical therapy, at least at the VA, if you show improvement they'll continue with therapy, but if you don't, then they will cease therapy. It makes sense really, I mean why spend time with people who aren't improving when you can better spend your time helping people who are improving. Initially it seemed counterintuitive that they would stop therapy on people not improving, but I get it now. So in my physical therapy, my goal was to increase my strength, improve my coordination, be able to stand, and be able to bend over to pick something up. Preferably by bending at the knees and not on my waist. In my OT assessment, my goals were to increase my hand strength and work on my dexterity. When I tested my grip strength, my left hand was slightly stronger than my right hand. I told the therapist that's because that's the hand I use for my remote control. Then I told her how Kelly (home OT) told me that if I wanted to work on developing my sense of pressure I could do so by picking up potato chips. I told Kelly, "Hell yeah I can do that, in fact if I have to, I'll eat twice as many just make sure I got it down right."

After my assessments I was scheduled for six more appointments each which would culminate on September 24th. That's if all went according to plan – and seriously, when does that ever happen?

Next on my stop was my old PT/OT stomping grounds. Mary wasn't there but Sandy was and also another nurse who I had known during my time in the hospital. I chatted with them for a little while and when they had get back to work I went on to my last stop of the day -Medical records. I stopped at the door of the woman's office because I was afraid if I got in there I would never get out, what with the scooter and all. She provided me with a release form to sign and then asked me what dates I wanted my record from and also if I wanted them on paper or disk. When she told me there were over 1000 documents for the four months I spent there, I elected to go with the disk. She told me she would compile it on Thursday, and send it off on Friday. I would have it the following week. I was elated.

When I got back to turn in my scooter at the desk I had them call a shuttle for me. The attendant who had issued me my scooter had attached a little American flag to my walker. That was sweet!

I did receive the disk with my medical records the next week but instead of 1000 documents it contained over 2000 documents. It took me the better part of a month to review the entire CD.

Part of the reason was because I was almost afraid to review it. After all, that was a dark time in my life. Once I delved into it I wouldn't review it for a day or so because it turned out to be depressing. But as I did review it, I determined that ultimately I needed to check it – all 2000 documents. As I went through it, I noted interesting events or milestones that I had achieved. I noted the date, the event, the results and most importantly the page number for easier reference in the future.

During the course of this undertaking, I finally had my physiatry exam in Ann Arbor. The trip down was uneventful and my scheduled appointment happened on time. I was told my exam would consist of a doctor reviewing my entire case from the beginning, to include my OT and PT progress, and that after an overview, they would decide if there was something that needed to be added or taken away. It was a review of medications as well. By this time I realized my medical records from the time I spent in the hospital was 2000 pages and I can't imagine what it must look like now with home-based care, a broken foot, a biopsy, and the list goes on. Therefore I was not surprised in the least when the doctor asked me for what I term a Reader's Digest version. After some review, questions, the limited physical exam regarding ataxia and neuropathy, he found my left ankle to be in need of some form of support. Potentially an ankle brace would be issued. He left the exam room to consult with another doctor. I met her and a resident when all three of them came back to the room. It was quite crowded in there. We discussed my options and an ankle brace was the end result. Fortunately they had one in stock, and after visiting prosthetics on the second floor I was outfitted within the hour. Then I had to wait the rest of the day for the others who came down on the shuttle with me to complete their appointments. I grabbed a hot dog and a bottle of water and took up my spot near the window next to the coffee pot where I had spent my time the previous month. A guy by the name of Dave sat down with me, or more accurately, at the same table that I was at. There were other seats available, but I suppose that if he were a regular I was probably sitting in his "spot". He made several phone calls while I sat there and I felt like I was intruding even though I had been there first. We talked a bit but then I got a phone call and I saw the driver go by, so I said my goodbyes and followed her. I met up with the woman who had sat closest to me on the shuttle down and we talked for the rest of the afternoon, sometimes being joined by another shuttle alumni. She and I discovered that we had a lot in common when it came to wanting to spend time by ourselves. I explained to her that since I had been off the home-based care program I now was able to have what I call, "people – free days". It's not that the people in my life aren't great, they are, but I like to be by myself and choose when I interact with others. For the longest time, I have had to depend on other people's kindness, for them to fit me into their schedule, to help me out whether it be shopping, cleaning the bathroom, and the other home-based care services or even simple things like vacuuming. My house is my refuge again, I love it, and I make no apologies for it. On the trip back, the three of us who had spent the afternoon chatting while waiting for the return shuttle, talked amongst ourselves about movies and TV shows and somehow this turned into a trivia game. It sure made time go fast though it probably annoyed the hell out of the other riders. During a rest stop, Diane saw there was a McDonald's a few stores down. She asked each of us if we wanted anything and we all declined. She came back 10 minutes later and had a hamburger for everyone on the bus including both drivers. She had an extra hamburger for anyone who wanted it. Yes, she had a taker, and no, it wasn't me.

As we left the shuttle we wished each other well and I told her maybe I'd see her again on another shuttle. Overall it was a pretty good day although it was long. We had gotten on the shuttle at 6 AM and returned at 5 PM. I called my neighbors to come pick me up and they joked with me on the phone asking me if I had gotten lost? She said, "I even asked Ray, are you sure you stayed by the phone all day?"

In the ensuing months, I would continually improve in both my OT and PT. My next round of OT was with my original OT, Mary. I was convinced, for a short time, that my PT person Paul was trying to kill me. He kept pushing my physical limits and that was a good thing. He would put me on the stationary bike for a period of time and he always advised me that if I needed to take break I could. I told him once that if I wanted to stop any therapy, just because I didn't want to do it, then I would not stop. However, if I needed to stop because I really could not do it, then I would not put myself in harm's way.

Sandy retired in November of 2015. I wrote her a little poem to remember me by and as my last weeks of PT/OT were winding down I gave a lot of consideration to the various techniques each of my therapists had employed. They were all amazing and good at what they do- they end up as cheerleaders- never letting you believe the impossible isn't, in fact, possible.

EPILOGUE

On March 5, 2016, two years to the day after I finished my stay at the VA hospital, I met with a 'friend of a friend' who had heard about my story. He was adamant about meeting me as he had also been stricken ill and exhibited the same symptoms as I.

I wasn't convinced that it was the same thing for a few reasons, 1. I hadn't met anyone who had even remotely the same thing, and 2. he seemed to have recovered from this affliction entirely. I was skeptical, to say the least, until we met that afternoon, sat together on my parents' lanai, and reviewed exactly what had happened to us – the onset, the deficiencies incurred, and the path to recovery.

He and I agreed to disagree about which of us had it worse (I feel his situation was worse due to the immediacy of his symptoms, and he feels mine was worse due to the extent of the residual deficiencies I still exhibit), but we definitely exhibited the same characteristics (neuropathy, unsteady balance; 'lizard vision') to varying degrees. He hasn't recovered entirely, but his progress is phenomenal, and he refuses to give up. I quickly discovered why he was eager to meet me. He told me that, out of the 200 other cases he had heard of, I was the only one he knew that survived.

We do share some background commonalities; we come from the same hometown; we both served the U.S. military in Turkey, and the onset occurred a few decades after our time in Turkey. Is it a coincidence? Perhaps.

Is it a coincidence that, of all of the people in this world, we found this bizarre common bond? Not likely.

A friend of mine said to me recently, "I'm glad you found him because he can relate to your struggle, the rest of us can empathize, but we haven't a clue."

She's right. Through this entire situation I've wanted people to understand my plight, but I never wanted to have them experience it in order to do so.

Each in our own way, during our recovery, we seek to survive and advance.

To paraphrase a quote by Edward Everett Hale, "I am only one person, but I AM one person.... there is much I can't do...but I CAN do...and I will not let that which I CANNOT do stop me from doing what I CAN do."

Author's note...shortly after I finished writing this, I was diagnosed with stage 3 colon cancer. Dealing with that, emotionally and physically, is the next adventure in what continues to be an unusual journey.

I'd Rather Be Me

My life has brought me uncertainty, pleasure and pain
Even so I've always known I had a lot to gain.
But with everything I have been through
I still have so much to do
And with everything I have yet to see
I know for certain in the end
I'd rather be me.
You, yourself, have so much to do
Possibly a lot to get through
But I know myself
And in the end
I'd rather be me, my friend.
ja '15

Poem for Mary

Mary,
What truly matters?
It is that you taught me
How to 'transfer'
So I could pee.
We had laughter
And we had fun...well not then. ;-)
But what you really sought
To teach me in the end
Was what would make me whole again...
Watching me eat on my own...
Driving my wheelchair w/o running anyone down-
(Ok, that doesn't really rhyme – but what the hell, I don't
do this for a living!)
You took me through my paces....
And watched me tie my own shoe laces.
When I look at my 'report card'
And witness all that I can do-
I thank God that he sent me back to you.
ja '15

Sandy's Poem

Thank you
For your service to me-
You weren't the person
I expected to see one morning
in my room when I pretended to be asleep
as I played dead
as I pulled up the covers
and put the pillow
over my head. ;-)
You were one of the first
to witness me literally
standing on my own again
'with much encouragement'
from you my friend.
You may not recall it again
but I, for one, won't ever forget it
in the end.
The experience of finally
standing alone on my own
is emblazoned in my memory.
This last part won't rhyme-
Sorry about kicking your shins
time after time...
but hell, Maytag
please remember me
cuz I will never forget you!
ja '15